PINNACLE OF THE PERRY BARR PETS
The Men and Matches Behind Villa's Double

by Simon Page

Juma

First published in 1997 by
Juma
Trafalgar Works
44 Wellington Street
Sheffield S1 4HD
Tel. 0114 272 0915
Fax. 0114 278 6550
Email: juma@mailhost.cityscape.co.uk

ISBN 1 872204 30 9

To

My parents and my Nan - for ensuring I followed a Claret & Blue path.

Dave Woodhall - for giving me a spleen venting outlet and much more.

And most of all

To Karen, Stacey and Kirsty - for being a constant reminder that there

are far more important things in life than football.

Acknowledgements

Thanks first and foremost to my father for his meticulous proof reading. Very much appreciated. If there are errors they are my fault. Cheers to Dave Woodhall. Without Heroes and Villains there is no way this book would have been written. To Andy Colquhoun who taught me more in two weeks than I've learnt in twenty-six years. And, of course, to Martin Lacey and Juma for publishing this tome.

Librarians (wonderful people that they are) have been of enormous help. Those who keep the records at Post & Mail House deserve special mention, not least for trusting me with some very delicate and irreplaceable objects. Similarly, the Birmingham Central Library Local History Department worked hard on my behalf, as did the most conscientious and persistent librarian of them all, Rosemary Prior at Birchfield. Andrew Cowie at Coloursport deserves thanks as well.

I would like, also, to express my gratitude to a number of people at the Birmingham Post and Mail, particularly; Phil Brown, Mark Woodward, Neil Moxley, Ian Willars, Rob Bishop, Sharon Sellway, Mike Ward, Adrian Milledge and Nigel Hastilow.

A number of people and organisations have provided help on many matters. To Steven Pennell, cheers for letting me share the fruits of your research and sorry for you know what! For delving into Jeremiah Griffiths' past, I'd like to thank Peter Aldridge and ask him how he knows so much. A big thank you also to Ian Rigby (authority on all things Prestonian), Liverpool FC, Blackburn Rovers FC, Preston North End FC, the Football Association and Dennis 'Trinity' Dudley of Messrs. Sue, Grabbit & Runne.

What can be said (other than the hundred-plus pages which follow) about the men whose stories are told in this book? I only wish I had the chance to see them play. They were fortunate enough to play for a Club whose history is rich enough for a million more books like this one. So the biggest thank you goes to Aston Villa FC for providing moments of ecstasy too numerous to mention.

Contents

Introduction

Birmingham's Number 91 bus route should hold a special place in the hearts of all Aston Villa fans. As it winds its way from the City Centre to the Pheasey, the bus traces the incredible rise to glory of the world famous football club. This geographical coincidence, one is sure, has resulted by accident rather than design, but for the claret and blue 'anorak' types it remains a step back into a past more glorious than the current generation could possibly dream of.

Having looped through Hockley, one reaches Villa Cross and the start of our - and the Villa's - story. As the driver steers his charge into Heathfield Road, strange physical and mental changes are experienced. Neck hairs rise in a salute to truly great men. Outside, the cars are replaced by carriages. Colourful 1990's clothes become the solemn dress of the Victorian era. Even the date on the ticket reads 1874. And the ugly sodium street lamps metamorphose into beautiful ornate gaslights.

It is under the glow of the first of these that four men stand. Walter Price, William Scattergood, Jack Hughes and Frederick Matthews - all members of the Aston Villa Wesleyan Chapel Cricket Team formed two years earlier - are discussing the possibilities of forming a football club. Little do they realise the force they are unleashing on world sport.

We leave the Christian sportsman behind, although only for the three minutes it takes to get to the other end of Heathfield Road. For on the right is Wilson Road, but it is not crowded with modern houses any more. Instead, thirty men are kicking a ball around a meadow. Having played the first half under Rugby Union rules, Aston Villa and Aston Brook St. Mary are now using the round ball. The cheer which greets Jack Hughes' winning goal can just be heard if one listens carefully enough.

The end of THE street has been reached. Sadly, owing to uninspired route planning by West Midlands Travel, the 91 turns left. Ploughing a straight course would have taken the time traveller to the Victorian Pleasure Park of the Aston Lower Grounds and Sir Thomas Holte's garden: Aston Park. Both were the scenes of very early Villa triumphs.

But no matter. As the driver tries to make up lost time with a Stirling Moss-type negotiation of the Perry Barr roundabout, certain passengers - while clinging on for dear life - look left. Some will see Leslie Road. Others spot the boundary of the famous Wellington Road enclosure, home of the 'Perry Barr Pets.' Meanwhile, the Old Crown & Cushion is the scene of great drunken revelry (some things never change). The talk is of two trophies. This is the story behind the revellers' joy.

* * *

How does one go from a church cricket team and occasional 'parks hackers' to the greatest, biggest, most successful and famous, football club in the world in the space of a mere twenty-three years? The answer, it would seem, lies in the perfect combination of five key elements: passion, luck, vision, planning and pure, raw talent. These ingredients produced 'Aston Villa' and the proof of its greatness is known as 'The Double.'

To begin at the beginning, passion was much in evidence within the gaslight group, all of whom lived by the 19th Century creed of Muscular Christianity. Such was their - and their comrades' - commitment that they would play in all weathers on atrocious strips of waste ground as they learned a new sport. It is a passion which many people falsely claim to possess today, although fortunately there are some men and women who can truly claim to have the claret and blue blood running through their veins. They are the select few who have inherited the Founding Four's dedication.

Then there is the luck element. The Gods must surely have decreed that, in 1876, George Burrell Ramsay should walk through Aston Park at the same moment that Aston Villa were holding a practice match. Such were the skills of the small Scotsman, who asked if he might join in, that he was immediately appointed captain, taught the Wesleyans how to play, and steered Villa to their greatest triumphs. He could have seen another club playing. The Villa flame may have flickered and died.

Similarly, what luck that the great Archie

Hunter never found his way to Calthorpe FC's ground. Had he have done so, they and not the Villa would have become the Midlands' premier team. It wasn't long before Calthorpe disappeared for ever, a fate that could have befallen the Lions. And what outside influences ensured that Frederick Rinder and William McGregor should come to work in Birmingham? Had Rinder stayed in his native Liverpool, it is likely that 10th April 1897 would have seen Everton defeat the Villa to lift the Double rather than the other way round, such was the value of this great man to the fortunes of his football club.

Luck, however, is of no use if it is not exploited to the full. This is where the incredible vision of the men behind the Club played such a big part in the rise of Aston Villa. Ramsay discovered and purchased the lease on the Perry Barr enclosure. McGregor first voiced his ideas for a League whilst at a Villa committee meeting at the Crown & Cushion, then went on to make it a reality. And Rinder. What didn't he do? He possessed so many qualities. The business acumen to maximise the Club's financial clout. The vision to form a limited Company which would transform the Aston Lower Grounds into the world's greatest sporting arena. And a strength of character best demonstrated when he called the infamous Barwick Street meeting, at which he swept away the men who were running Villa into the ground.

These three men were masters of planning. McGregor organised his League and, on a more local scale, the transport of Villa's army of travelling support. Rinder looked after the finances. And Ramsay built a squad of greats. From the low of Barwick Street to the ultimate glory at Crystal Palace five years later, a team was pieced together in the manner of a jigsaw; each section fitting together perfectly and complementing the whole. The story of the construction of the Class of '97 is almost as worthy of telling as the story of the season itself. For this is the tale of the fifth great element: pure, raw talent. Ramsay got Villa an abundance of it.

By Christmas 1890, Jas Cowan - the greatest centre-half of his day - was already a fixture in the Villa side. Jas was yet another Scotsmen lured to Brum, and when George Ramsay heard about the ex-Third Lanark star, he kidnapped him. Well, that may be taking it a little far but it is true to say that Cowan, who like Archie Hunter before him had been looking for a different football team, was not allowed to leave Ramsay's presence until he had signed for the Villa.

The Yuletide of 1890 saw Ramsay give the fans a truly wondrous present: Charlie Athersmith. The fastest man in football was about to be unleashed on unsuspecting and largely innocent League defences. He was joined two months later by John Devey, the man who would captain two Cup winning teams and five League Champions in eight years at the helm. It is fitting that these two should join almost in tandem, for their partnership on the right wing betrayed an almost telepathic understanding of each other's movements .

1892 may have been a quiet one in terms of transfers with only Bob Chatt and Frank Burton of the Double squad arriving. These had lesser parts to play in the ultimate glory that lay ahead but were important reserves none the less. But, the year was hugely significant elsewhere, for it saw Barwick Street, which has been briefly mentioned, and also Villa's lowest point. Can there be many clubs which at any stage in their history could claim that losing a Cup Final was their nadir? Humiliation at the hands of bitter rivals West Bromwich Albion was, however, the great turning point.

A season of consolidation took the Club to the summer 1893 and four Ramsay signings which drastically improved every section of the team. In defence, left-back James Welford arrived. His career would see him make history and have the worst disciplinary record in the Club, so often did he fall foul of the strict regulations laid down by the Committee. The West Brom Cup winning team was raided with John Reynolds being the booty. His half-back play earned him caps for England and Ireland and made him a Villa legend. Up front, the left wing was bolstered by Steve Smith, another future International. The result of these transfers? Villa won the League for the first time.

But there is still one 1893 signing yet to be mentioned. Of all the greats who George Ramsay lured to Aston Villa, one man stands out from the rest although he is cruelly over-looked even by Villa historians. That man was poached from the frighteningly-titled Middlesbrough Ironopolis club. His name was Joe Grierson and he had the single honour of coaching every one of Aston Villa's League Championship winning sides until the triumvirate of Ron Saunders, Tony Barton and Roy McClaren took the Club to glory in 1981. Under trainer Grierson, the League was conquered six times and the FA Cup four times in a run of success which it took a World War to halt. Not until Shankly and Paisley led Liverpool to the peaks was that level of domination eclipsed anywhere in the world.

The day-to-day running of the team was now under the control of George Ramsay, Joe Grierson and John Devey; three men who knew that one shouldn't rest on one's laurels. Already, the Villa had become enough of a giant that a single League Championship would not suffice. In the summer of '94, Tom Wilkes was brought in to keep goal and his job was made easier by the acquisition of the 'Prince of Full-Backs.' Howard Spencer would become not only the greatest right-back in the world, but also a fine Villa captain and later a club director.

But 1894/5 - his first season in the League - was 'disappointing.' The Villa only finished third! This was more than made up for, however, by revenge over the old enemy. The knee of John Devey (not Bob Chatt as has often been written) propelled the ball into the Albion net after just 30 seconds and the FA Cup was back in Brum... well, at least until it was stolen from Shillcock's shop window.

But back to the League. In '94/5, Villa had been beaten only once at home. The following season, with four new recruits, they would drop just one point at Perry Barr. And win their second championship. That 1895/6 season saw the debuts of Jeremiah Griffiths and the great Scottish centre forward John Campbell, whose eye for goal was matched only by his precision passing. John Cowan came down to join his brother Jas and to do battle with Steve Smith for the outside left position. The fourth of the quartet was the matchless James Crabtree. The most versatile footballer of his era, he would eventually play in all five 'back' positions for England. For the Villa, he was a handy emergency centre forward too.

As the '95/6 campaign drew to a close, Ramsay et al were already preparing for even greater glories. Young Albert Evans had been secured early in the season as a partner for Spencer at the back. Grimsby were paid a record fee for a goalkeeper bringing Jimmy Whitehouse to the Midlands. The relegated Small Heath club received the world record transfer fee for their star forward, and expert cricketer, Fred Wheldon. The purchase of goalkeeper Billy George completed the squad building.

The jigsaw was finished. The scene was set for Aston Villa's greatest triumph. But spare a thought for Dennis Hodgetts. After ten years, 215 games and 91 goals for the Claret and Blues, he had rightly won a place in the Villa hall of fame. Yet on the eve of the Double season, he accepted Small Heath's offer to become their captain. Right up until his death - and he lived into his eighties - Dennis never stopped regretting that decision.

Having won the League in '96, the Villa wound down with a tour of the North. In the space of five days they played games against Hibernian, Celtic (the Scottish Champions), Ayr and Newcastle, before returning to Birmingham to prepare for the slaughter of Stoke in the replay of the Staffordshire Cup Final. That victory brought a record fifth win in the competition. One by one the players re-signed

for the Club with the main press speculation, and worry for the supporters, being a few scurrilous stories linking Charlie Athersmith with a move to Everton.

Off the field, work on the Aston Lower Grounds - which would become Villa Park - was going on apace and the Club announced that the playing surface would be given a year to set before being put to use. Those familiar with the stadium's recent pitch problems would be forgiven for wishing such action could be repeated today.

1896 had seen four trophies won by the Villa (the Birmingham Senior Cup and the Birmingham and District League Championship being the other two). Such was the weight of expectation carried by the Club, however, that the *Birmingham Daily Post* saw fit to publish the following - some may say prophetic - words on 4th May 1896:

"We trust that next season will be even more successful and we shall have the pleasure of seeing the League Cup and English Cup side by side."

1896/7 saw only half the trophy wins of the preceding campaign, yet it was a glorious year the like of which has never been bettered. The campaign represented the pinnacle of the Club affectionately known as 'The Perry Barr Pets'.

Chapter One

In The Beginning

On Monday 17th August, 1896, the Villa players began pre-season training. The summer had seen a fair amount of speculation regarding the club, as well as one or two notable occasions for some of the players. John Campbell had resisted the temptation to return to Celtic; James Crabtree had finally succumbed to the Board's pressure to re-sign. The stories linking Charlie Athersmith with a move to Everton (transfer rumours were extremely rife even in those days) had proved false while, on a happier note, a truly claret and blue affair was thrown in celebration of Jas Cowan's marriage. Meanwhile, Jimmy Welford had scored his maiden century for Warwickshire at Leicester. All that was left to do was prepare the squad in readiness for improving on last season's League Championship triumph.

The team's practice matches were regularly attended by two to three thousand spectators, such was the Villa's pulling power. The higher figure would be a conservative estimate of the crowd which turned up for the final public training session on Thursday 24th August to watch twenty-two of the Villa squad 'play for their places.'

The names of the two teams that day gave some slight indication of the Committee's likely selection for the opening match against Stoke City. The 'Probables' took on the 'Improbables' with the former cruising to a 4-0 victory. It must, surely, have been soul-destroying to see one's name under the heading 'Improbable.' It would seem that subtlety hardly existed in abundance at Perry Barr.

The line-ups were:
Probables: Wilkes, Spencer, Welford, Reynolds, Jas Cowan, Crabtree, Athersmith, Wheldon, Devey, Campbell, John Cowan.
Improbables: Whitehouse, Evans, Bourne, Griffiths, Chatt, Burton, Woodfall, Flannagan, Rideout, Harvey, Smith.

Rather unsurprisingly, after the match the Committee announced that the 'Probables' had become the 'Definites' and would open Villa's campaign. Whilst five of the vanquished side would not figure in first-team action again, Jimmy Whitehouse, Albert Evans and Steve Smith would all become regulars in a great Villa line-up.

Before the season proper begins, it is worth noting that, despite having paid a record fee for a goalkeeper (Whitehouse) and then leaving him out of the starting eleven, the day of the 'Probably' game coincided with the first reports of Billy George signing. He would eventually go on to become a legend between the sticks for the Villa. Three great 'keepers; not bad in any era!

At 5:30 pm on Wednesday 2nd September, around 6,000 people cheered as John Devey rolled the ball to John Campbell. The Perry Barr Pets' 1896/7 season had got under way at Wellington Road against Stoke, a side the Villa had only lost to once in fourteen League meetings. The home team unveiled a new and, as it turned out, short-lived central forward combination with Wheldon at inside right, Devey in the middle, and Campbell partnering John Cowan down the left channel. Early on in this game, however, both wings appeared to be operating well. The passing between Wheldon and Athersmith was particularly eye catching.

The first half was played almost entirely at the visitors end. Attack after attack kept goalkeeper Latham busy and, as was inevitable, Villa finally made the breakthrough after twenty minutes. John Cowan received the ball from Campbell some 20 yards out and crashed a low drive past the despairing stretch of Latham's left hand.

Villa continued to press. The right flank of Reynolds, Wheldon and Athersmith bemused the Stoke rear-guard. This caused the visitors to pack their left side only for sweeping passes to pick out Campbell or John Cowan on the left. Sadly, these two were shooting abysmally. Despite having golden opportunities presented them by the awesome passing from the right, shot after shot went high or wide. At last, though, Campbell forced Latham to make a save. The Villa forward shot through a crowded area and the 'keeper could only punch the ball out to John Devey who made no mistake.

Fred Wheldon continued to harass the Stoke backs with a fine display of the art of dribbling as Villa completely dominated proceedings. Stoke managed the odd breakaway but it was left to their half-backs to attempt long-shots which never troubled Wilkes.

The second half too followed the same script with the 'Pets' pressing, only for the final shots to fly harmlessly away from Latham's charge. When the custodian was occasionally called into action, he showed why many regarded him as the finest 'Number 1' in the country. But with ten minutes left, and completely against the run of play, the visitors pulled one back through Baird. The centre forward made the only positive connection with the ball during a goalmouth scramble. The game finally resembled a contest as play swung from end to end but Villa held out to take a 2-1 victory and both points.

Three days later it was time to make the short journey to the sloping pitch at Stoney Lane where the Lions took on their oldest and most bitter of rivals, West Bromwich Albion. The result should have been a foregone conclusion. In '95/6, the Baggies had finished bottom of Division One but managed to retain their status following the Test Matches (a similar system to today's Play-Offs). The Champions vs. arguably the poorest side in the Division? No contest.

But, as all football fans know, derby matches have an annoying habit of ignoring the form book. This football quirk was particularly in evidence at Stoney Lane where matches against the Villa could turn very nasty indeed. Often, the two sets of supporters would head to the ground with pockets full of stones to hurl at one another and the local constabulary were in a state of red-alert whenever the fixture came round. Yes, hooliganism was around 100 years ago and, whilst it wasn't as widespread as certain eras have known it to be, some of the antics of 'Victorian Thug' would cause even the most crazed of 1980's hooligan to wince.

The 1896/7 meeting between the two enemies was not marred by overtly violent scenes, although the atmosphere could hardly be described as pleasant. The locals were no doubt less prone to show the traditional welcome to their Brummie visitors thanks to their team's second half performance.

The Villa began playing up the slope with the wind in their favour and dominated Albion with ease. It was plain to see which club possessed the greater talent. A lovely move, typical of the unique Villa style, gave the visitors a deserved half-time lead. Athersmith received a pass in the centre circle. With one touch he laid it through to Wheldon who again only needed one touch to pick out Devey. The skipper shot first time on the turn and beat Reader, the Albion 'keeper, easily. It was flowing football so like that which is praised today; a style which the Villa pioneered.

Something must have happened to the players during the interval because they were not the same team in the second half. Albion used their kick and rush style to great effect while the Villa couldn't string two passes together. With fifteen minutes left, Welford handled the ball and Williams beat Whitehouse (who had come in for the mysteriously dropped Tom Wilkes) with the spot kick, thus sending the majority of the 12,000 crowd wild. The Villa had gone to pieces. Jas Cowan and Welford were not at the races, whilst proof that Spencer and Reynolds had lost their way came when West Brom's left wing conjured up two more goals to give the victory to the home side.

That defeat left Villa in a lowly ninth place in the first League table of the new campaign. A greater shock was at the top where the Albion sat with maximum points from two games. A truer reflection of the merits of the two teams came, of course, with the final placings. The defeat at Stoney Lane, which some may put down to the 'levelling' factor of derby games, was no less unforgivable. To let WBA score three was a nightmare. They only scored another 30 in the rest of the season making them lowest scorers for the year. A poor side - not for the last time in '96/7 - had humiliated the Kings of English Football.

Before the Villa could attempt to right the wrongs of Stoney Lane, a friendly match was played at Second Division Grimsby. Four thousand people saw an entertaining 3-3 draw in which Fred Wheldon scored twice and Jimmy Welford popped up from his left-back position to notch up a rare strike. Despite this, the trip was not a happy one for Welford, nor Whitehouse. It is not known exactly what the two players did, but whatever it was the Committee felt it necessary to drop them both for: *"disregard of discipline."* Welford, as has already been mentioned, was no stranger to those words.

So a changed Villa line-up - for the third time in three games - took to the Wellington Road pitch on 12th September to take on a strong Sheffield United outfit. The Villa team to emerge from the Blacksmith's Yard changing rooms was:

Wilkes, Spencer, Crabtree (the versatile!), Reynolds, Jas Cowan, Burton, Athersmith, Wheldon, Devey, Campbell, John Cowan.

A disappointingly low turnout of 5,000 came with the expectation of a Villa win. This turned out to be United's last chance of securing an elusive victory at Perry Barr; definitely their bogey ground. The visitors were known for their strong defence - the best in the League that season - but the smart money was on Villa's forwards to upset the miserly Yorkshire backs.

What the crowd saw was a scrappy game in which neither side performed with credit. The Villa had a system of play in which they had total faith, but this sometimes frustrated supporters and commentators alike. Newspaper reports of this match bemoaned Villa's determination to play pretty, intricate football when a more *"vigorous onslaught"* would have been - in the general consensus - the more profitable route.

The individual superiority of the Villa players got them into good positions but, when the shooting wasn't wild, Foulkes in goal was on top of his game. The forwards weren't working well as a unit and the cross-field balls which had been the hallmark of the '95/6 campaign were simply not in evidence. At half-time, the teams shared two goals, Frank Burton opening his account for the season. After the interval, Devey reorganised his front rank. The skipper moved to inside right, Wheldon took up his more familiar inside left role and Campbell came into the middle. It didn't pay instant dividends but the feeling amongst the 'experts' was that the switch would work in time.

Athersmith managed to get away down the right and centred perfectly for Wheldon to head Villa in front. But Priest levelled the scores again and Villa, thanks to sterling play by John Reynolds and James Crabtree, repelled the United attacks which persisted almost without response right to the end. Neither the game nor the performance were well received. The press questioned whether the Villa were suffering from a decadence which only personnel changes could rectify. Three - admittedly disappointing - games into the season and already the team was being slated. The *Birmingham Daily Post* commented: *"A miracle will be needed if Aston Villa are to escape defeat at Everton on Saturday."*

* * *

The trip to Goodison was the first chance for Villa's impressive travelling support to make a 'decent' excursion. Away matches nearly always saw between 500 and 2,000 Brummies take advantage of the 'specials' which the one and only William McGregor would arrange. For this game, as well as the straight 'there and back' package, three and four day mini-breaks were laid on courtesy of the London and North West Railway Company. The Villa knew the value of a good following away from home and McGregor, ever the visionary, ensured it was as easy as possible for the fans to travel.

It was a huge following that left New Street for Liverpool on 19th September. Yet owing to the Villa's indifferent start (they were in eleventh place going into the game at second place Everton) the pundits were all predicting a home win. As any Villa fan will confirm, however, one should never try to predict what the Claret and Blue will do.

Whitehouse had returned from the dog-house to replace Wilkes but the outfield players were the same as those who had performed with such mediocrity against Sheffield United. Devey kept the same forward combination which began that game, rather than persevere with his second half switch.

Everton played in a similar, if less polished, style to the Villa. This meant that the Villa's system worked well against the Liverpudlians where it had failed a week earlier. The press grudgingly accepted this fact after the match, yet still expressed a desire for Devey's men to be more direct against the more basic tactics of other teams. Philistines! The fact was that, in a stormer of a game, the incredible inter-play between the visiting players was not only a joy to behold, but a nightmare for opposing defenders.

Villa won the game 3-2 thanks to the fact that the Everton full-backs, Barker and Storrier, could not begin to counter the mesmerising skills of Athersmith and John Cowan who simply tore their enemies to pieces. Meanwhile, down the middle Devey and Campbell were finding acres of space by dropping deep. This policy reaped rich rewards as a 2-0 half-time lead was recorded through first Devey, then Campbell having time to control the ball before unleashing ferocious long shots which flashed into the net.

Everton pulled one back on 65 minutes but almost immediately Campbell was gifted the third. A fairly strong shot from the Scotsman's right boot appeared to be going wide until it caught Storrier a glancing blow; just enough to steer it in off the post. Campbell claimed it and was credited with it. The home side managed to pull one back through the individual flair of Milward, but Villa cruised to victory. Whitehouse, Spencer, Crabtree and Reynolds formed a brick wall which Everton, despite having at least half the possession, found less generous than their own backs had been. Thus the Villa won for the first time ever at Goodison before a massive 25,000 fans.

In the freak world of early-season League tables, when Everton came to Perry Barr the following Saturday to contest the return fixture, Villa had jumped to sixth and the visitors were down in ninth place. The win at Goodison had given Villa fans confidence of collecting the two points but, as it was foolish to write them off a week previous, so the unpredictability of the 'Pets' was shown to a 20,000 strong Brummie crowd.

For the first time in two years and four days, Aston Villa lost at home. As with their last defeat, 2-1 was the scoreline after the visitors took rather better than Villa to the slippery Perry Barr surface.

Crabtree played in his third position in five games. He started at right-back because Spencer was allowed time away owing to a bereavement. This paved the way for a return for bad boy Welford while Burton retained his place at left-half. The match, like the Goodison game, proved evenly contested between two teams which would have even today's 'purists' drooling. Villa enjoyed more of the possession but Everton gave a solid demonstration of the counter-attacking art.

In the 16th minute, John Cowan played a reverse pass inside from the left. It fell perfectly into the stride of Devey who calmly placed the ball past Briggs. To the Villa fans - and no doubt any neutrals in the crowd - the script was being followed perfectly. Three minutes later and those same observers knew they had a game on. Welford gave the Committee a footballing, rather than disciplinary, reason to drop him when he inexplicably lunged at a very tame shot from Hartley. Whitehouse was left stranded and Everton had been gifted an equaliser.

Welford had a truly awful game. Eventually, he and Crabtree swapped places and the latter carried his partner throughout the ninety minutes. With Villa effectively playing with one man - albeit Crabtree - at the back, Everton always looked the more dangerous combination. They got their reward in the 82nd minute when Chadwick burst through to clinch the points.

It was not just at the back that Villa had problems. Up front their shooting continued to be of an extremely low standard. An added difficulty came from the lack of good crosses, which was highly un-Villa-like. Service to Athersmith was virtually nil whilst on the other wing, John Cowan put centre after centre uselessly behind the front-line. On an otherwise fruitless, though entertaining, day, only news that some 'experts' had decreed that Charlie Athersmith was the world's fastest player seemed to offer any comfort to the Club. A night of tossing and turning then!

Next up was the first of what would be three trips to Bramall Lane this season. This was, however, the only time the Villa would play visitors to Sheffield United. 3rd October saw 40,000 fans pay £1,150 for the privilege of seeing Everton win the Merseyside derby at Goodison. Meanwhile across the Pennines, a rather more sedate 12,000 watched unbeaten United attempt to go one better than the draw at Perry Barr and repeat last season's feat of taking three points off the Villa. But for Whitehouse and the backs, that would have been what happened.

In a slight drizzle and on a marginally heavy pitch, both teams commendably stuck to their normal games. The thing is, for the first half hour, only United were any good at the 'normal' game. It was one-way traffic but the only time the home team found the Villa net, it was ruled out for a foul on Whitehouse.

Otherwise, the backs were in great form, thanks in no small part to the return of Spencer in place of the out-of-sorts Welford. It was not the same story up front where, until the last quarter of an hour of the first half, no meaningful attack took place. Even in that period up to the interval, only one weak Athersmith header forced Foulkes to make a save.

Five minutes after the break, Priest scored for the home team only to see it ruled offside. This stung Villa into life and suddenly, having spent the game very much on the back foot, they launched an incessant bombardment of the home goal. For nearly half an hour Whitehouse watched as, in the distance, Foulkes was called upon to make save after save. Twice Wheldon and once John Cowan saw goal-bound shots plucked from the air by one of the most agile 'keepers around.

In the last ten minutes, the match became a real ding-dong affair. The Villa showed all the pretty combination but Sheffield looked the more dangerous. Each time the home fans thought they may see a breakthrough though, there was the undoubted man-of-the-match Jas Cowan. He was a rock at centre-half and, in the first half especially, did so much to keep his side on level terms.

Another reason for the goalless scoreline was the whistle-happy referee - a football tradition that has lasted far too long. Play was by no means rough yet there was free-kick after free-kick, many of them resulting from what the ref saw as foul charges on Whitehouse. A 'keeper receiving so much protection was indeed a rare sight in 1896.

* * *

Two days later, the Club paid tribute to their skipper. Derby were the visitors at Perry Barr for John Devey's benefit match. Even on a cold and wet Monday, the attendance of 1,500 was disappointingly low and meant Devey would only net around £200.

The game itself was well-contested. Albert Evans, Bob Chatt and Steve Smith all played and, thanks in part to some fine play and also to Derby losing a man early on, Villa took a 2-0 lead into the break through strikes by Devey and Wheldon. In the second half Stevenson pulled one back for Derby but the Villa held on comfortably. The home team's wingers were particularly outstanding and Steve Smith gave the Committee a reminder of his talents with an awesome display.

All of which set the team up nicely for the return fixture with West Brom. Revenge was an added incentive (if any were needed) to put one over their neighbours. Welford returned to left-back allowing Crabtree to slot back into his favoured left-half position. The unlucky man to lose out was Frank Burton who had shown up well in four consecutive appearances. Albion had improved on last season's performances; going into the match, the two West Midlands giants occupied the middle two places in the table with Villa, in 8th place, just ahead of their rivals. The Baggies had won only once in the League at Perry Barr before today and their hosts were in no mood to allow them to double that figure.

The star of the show was Fred Wheldon. He was in the inside-left position as Devey again tried himself at number 8 and Campbell down the middle. It worked perfectly. Wheldon, who had hardly set the world ablaze since his record transfer, rampaged through the Albion defence. On 20 minutes he received the ball in midfield, went on a mazey run which took him past three opponents and crashed a shot past a bemused Reader. The ball smacked the inside of the post and nestled in the net.

It was a brilliant finish to an incredible dribble and the goal galvanised the Villa forwards. Reader had no time to rest as shot after thundering shot rained in on his goal. Athersmith and Devey combined marvellously and the former's crosses wreaked havoc in the Albion defence. One of these found the crown of John Campbell who headed powerfully past Reader to give Villa a 2-0 half-time lead.

In the second period, the Villa had a strong wind behind them and simply penned the visitors back. Time after time they carved out wonderful opportunities and then wasted them with poor shooting. This was a problem which had inexplicably dogged them since the opening match. Twice Athersmith carried the ball half the length of the pitch before shooting wildly when a pass inside would have left Campbell with the goal at his mercy. On the other wing, John Cowan wasted a couple of chances after he had well and truly 'skinned' the Albion's right side.

But it is hard to pick fault after Wheldon's goal. The press claimed it was a reminder of a couple of season's ago when Fred was the best player in the country. Much of the success of the forwards in this match must, however, be attributed to the halfbacks who tackled strongly and fed the front line with perfect passes all game. Welford had his best game of the season although, to be fair, neither he nor Spencer and Whitehouse had an awful lot to do, such was Villa's dominance.

Thus 18,000 fans saw the most important game of the season won. The Albion had been vanquished. Before the match, a mere 0.02 difference in goal average separated the two sides. For ninety minutes on 10th October, that gap seemed like a gaping chasm. It wasn't just the win that pleased the Villa fans, it was the style and ease with which it was attained that made victory over the old enemy so much sweeter.

* * *

Seven games into the season for Villa and the League was beginning to settle down. Inconsistency and poor shooting was the pessimist's view of the 'Pets' but the signs were there, in some at times truly stunning play, that other teams ignored the Villa threat at their peril. Aston Villa found themselves in a highly mediocre seventh place in the table which looked like this:

| | | pld | home | | | | | away | | | | | | |
			w	d	l	f	a	w	d	l	f	a	g.av	pts
1	Bolton	7	3	1	0	6	1	2	1	0	6	3	3.00	12
2	Sheff U	6	2	1	0	4	0	1	2	0	7	5	2.20	9
3	Liverpool	8	2	1	1	5	2	2	0	2	5	5	1.43	9
4	Blackburn	7	3	0	1	9	4	0	2	1	2	4	1.38	8
5	Preston	6	3	0	0	13	7	0	2	1	2	4	1.36	8
6	Everton	6	2	0	1	6	5	2	0	1	4	3	1.25	8
7	**Aston Villa**	**7**	**2**	**1**	**1**	**7**	**5**	**1**	**1**	**1**	**4**	**5**	**1.10**	**8**
8	Sheff W	7	2	1	1	8	6	1	0	2	3	6	0.92	7
9	Burnley	7	2	2	0	6	4	0	0	3	5	9	0.85	6
10	W Brom	7	1	1	4	4	1	1	2	3	6	0.70	6
11	N Forest	5	1	1	0	6	2	0	2	1	3	6	1.13	5
12	Derby	6	2	1	1	13	9	0	0	2	0	3	1.08	5
13	Wolves	7	1	1	2	3	4	1	0	2	7	6	1.00	5
14	Stoke	6	1	0	1	4	4	1	0	3	6	11	0.67	4
15	Bury	6	0	1	1	1	2	1	0	3	3	10	0.33	3
16	Sunderland	8	0	1	2	1	5	0	2	3	4	10	0.33	3

Bolton and Sheffield United sat at the top unbeaten whilst last season's Second Division Champions Liverpool (who had replaced Small Heath in the top flight following the Test Matches) had adjusted to the higher level well. Villa's next opponents, Derby County, were scoring very well at home but had yet to record a strike away. The most important thing for all the clubs, and Villa in particular, was not to let anyone build a big lead. Villa were already four points off the pace and needed to string a few wins together.

Chapter Two

None Shall Pass
Goalkeepers and Full-backs

The Villa had a formidable defence in 1896/7. The two Sheffield clubs had marginally better goals against tallies but there were few forwards who wanted to tangle with the 'Pets' rear guard. Uniquely in Victorian football, the Villa full-backs were expected to pass the ball out of defence at every opportunity. The wild 'hoofs' upfield favoured by so many backs would soon see a player departing Perry Barr. This policy occasionally backfired and allowed the opposition a chance, but that was rare. Far more common was the sight of a well directed pass to the half-backs which would set the team on an unstoppable forward course.

As we have just seen, the Villa had kept two consecutive clean sheets; their first of the campaign. After a shaky start, the odd leak at the back had been plugged and the side were becoming much harder to score against. Indeed, they would not concede more than two in a single game again until December. It may not sound a great achievement but in the '96/7 campaign, an average of 3.13 goals were recorded in each game, yet breaches of the Villa's defence averaged only 1.27 per match.

Tom Wilkes began the season as first choice 'keeper, a luxury he had enjoyed since joining the Club in the summer of 1894. He arrived from Redditch Town as the Committee looked to improve a problem area for successive Villa teams. Jimmy Warner, who kept goal for six years, had left following the humiliating 3-0 Cup Final reversal at the hands of West Brom, a defeat which most fans blamed on the unfortunate custodian. To this day, rumours persist that Warner influenced the result to help to clear his gambling debts.

After he'd left in suspicious circumstances, Bill Dunning came in for a couple of seasons before Wilkes made the number 1 spot his own. Two incredibly successful campaigns followed as Wilkes kept a clean sheet in the 1895 Cup Final (again against the Albion) and then added a League Championship medal the following year. But despite his obvious skills, and even though he began '96/7 as first choice, the arrival of Jimmy Whitehouse spelt the end of Tom's Villa career. He never let the Club down in 57 League and Cup appearances but only sporadic call-ups ensued until, in 1899, Stoke moved in for him

* * *

The purchase of Whitehouse, at a time when Villa had a perfectly good 'keeper anyway, showed just how seriously the Committee viewed the position. Jimmy was a fine shot-stopper, although he never made the International grade despite being one of the best goalies around.

Tom Wilkes

Jimmy Whitehouse

It was in the summer of 1896 that a record £200 fee for a 'keeper winged its way to Grimsby as Jimmy Whitehouse travelled in the opposite direction. Even in the most one-sided games of the era, it was rare that any team didn't enjoy a period of sustained pressure and it is interesting to note from match reports how often Whitehouse saved his team in the most spectacular manner. Agile and possessing a great theoretical knowledge of the art of goal-keeping, Whitehouse showed nerves of steel to keep a rampaging Everton side at bay in a Cup Final which we shall shortly hear a great deal about.

For all his strengths, and the price tag he carried, Whitehouse only lasted two seasons and 43 appearances at the Villa before he was transferred to Newton Heath. The reason that he was made surplus to requirements was first announced on 27th August 1896

Earlier in the year, the Villa had played a friendly against a Bristol and District Select XI. In goal for the opponents was a 6' 1" man-mountain named Billy George who, when not on Army duties, stood his imposing 16 stone frame between Trowbridge Town's sticks. His transfer to Villa broke certain FA rules and saw George, Rinder and Ramsay all suspended for a month. He was worth it though. One of football's characters and the latest in a long line of Villa all-rounders (his debut for Warwickshire CCC against the South Africans saw him face five balls; three went for four runs, one for six and the fifth got him out) Billy missed out on Double glory.

That was bad luck but he made up for it in later years. When he retired just four games short of his 400th Villa match he possessed two Championship medals (and played a part in a third title winning campaign), three League runners-up medals and a Cup Winners medal from the 1905 defeat of Newcastle. This strength in depth of Villa's goalkeeping department began a tradition which is maintained to this day in the shape of Mark Bosnich and Michael Oakes. Villa don't always have the best custodians (Sam Hardy being the most notable exception) but they do like to possess a couple of very high quality ones.

* * *

An advantage which Wilkes, Whitehouse and - later - George had was the exceptional full-backs who protected them. Again, Villa had high quality players to fill this vital area. Even when injury depleted the squad, there was always Crabtree who could step into either full-back position; something he did seven times during this historic season.

James Welford

The campaign began with James Welford filling the left-back spot. Born in Glasgow in 1872, he moved to Birmingham twenty years later to join Mitchell St George a year after John Devey had left that very club for the Villa. Twelve months on and he was beginning a four year spell under Devey at Perry Barr.

He somewhat under-achieved at the Villa. His talent was legendary and when on top of his game it is doubtful there were any better. But he enjoyed the high life and, as has already been indicated, his penchant for over-indulging on Club tours got him into trouble with the Villa Committee. Later in the season, he would face the disciplinarian's wrath when left in Brum while the rest of the first-team went off to a training camp.

As with all full-backs, Welford did not count goal scoring amongst his greatest attributes. His one strike for the Villa though was a belter. In appaling weather he hit a 20 yard thunderbolt in Villa's 2-0 win over Bolton in December '95. Where he did have a demonstrated talent, however, was on the cricket field. The summer of 1896 saw him make his debut for Warwickshire. In his third game he scored a fine 118 and also took his first wicket in county cricket.

Welford did far better than most players in terms of medals won: 1893/4 League Championship medal, '94/5 FA Cup Winners medal, and '95/6 Championship medal again. But in Villa's greatest season he played only 10 games. This prompted Celtic to bid for his services as part of a triple raid on the Villa squad during the summer of '97. Celtic's policy paid dividends as they won the Scottish Championship the following year.. Another year later, Welford picked up a Scottish Cup medal before moving to Belfast Celtic in 1899. There, the Irish Cup was won and he thus became the second footballer to win that trio of Cup medals. The first will be revealed later!

His playing career was ended by injury whilst playing for Belfast at the age of 33. He moved back to Scotland where he died in 1940. His place in history had been assured and he helped Villa claim their place too.

* * *

Welford's slot in the Villa team was taken by the young star of the side. Albert Evans had the dubious honour of being the lowest paid regular member of the first-team squad. He received a

Albert Evans

weekly wage of 35 shillings, but all the money in the world could not have matched this man's incredible life story.

Born in Barnard Castle, County Durham, Evans, whilst on holiday in Brum, was introduced to Villa by Bob Chatt. 1896/7 season marked his debut for the Club as a 21 year old. He lined up alongside the great Howard Spencer (more of whom later) to form one of the youngest full-back partnerships in the Club's history. And what a partnership it was, arguably better than those 20th Century greats, Smart and Mort or Cummings and Callaghan.

For ten seasons he proudly wore the claret and blue and would no doubt have added to his 203 appearances but for being decidedly injury prone. Three times he broke his leg at the Villa, once when inexplicably jumping into a ditch during training! But it didn't take long for the Villa committee to realise what a solid left-back they had in 1896. Evans was a quick learner. As has already been mentioned, full-backs in his day tended to clear their lines quickly with a giant punt downfield. This

would have been Evans' favoured method of defence but for the intervention of Jas Cowan who would tell the new recruit to play a pass to James Crabtree or the other half-backs whenever possible.

Crabtree himself was another great mentor for young Albert who claimed that it was *"the easiest job in the world"* playing behind the Villa's versatile left-half. While the right side of the team understandably had much praise heaped upon it, the interplay between Evans and Crabtree on the left was an education to watch and turned many sticky moments into speedy, exhilarating attacks.

Despite all his success at Perry Barr and Villa Park, Evans never won a full cap, although he played for England against several European countries and represented the Football League in 1901 against Ireland. He also had the honour of occasionally captaining Villa. He was never permanently appointed skipper, instead understudying for both Devey and Spencer.

In 1906 he moved to West Brom. There, on Christmas Day 1908, he broke his leg for a fourth time and despite trying to come back, was forced to retire the following summer when he was offered a coaching post at The Hawthorns. That didn't spell the end of Albert's leg worries as a fifth fracture was sustained in a friendly match in 1915.

After serving in the First World War, Evans had a four year spell as Coventry manager which began in 1920. Following his resignation, he went off round the world trying his hand at a number of jobs including gold mining in the Yukon. His wanderlust satisfied, he returned to the Midlands and became a Villa scout, a post he filled until his death at home in Coventry in 1966, making him the last surviving member of the Double winning side. His final public appearance came in 1957 when he joined a banquet to celebrate Villa's seventh FA Cup triumph.

Evans, like so many Villa players of all eras, retained a special love for the Club; more proof - if more were needed - of the saying *"Once a Villa man always a Villa man."* Memories of his time at his Club were always close at hand for Albert. Pride of place in his living room was given over to a massive framed picture of the great Double team. He also kept a box containing over 40 medals won during his career including the three League Championships and one Cup winners gongs he gained with Villa and a commemorative gold medal for the Double event.

Evans claimed, probably falsely, that in all the time he was at the Club not one player ever handed in a transfer request. Regardless of the veracity of that statement, it was true that the Villa looked after their players incredibly well and the spirit and atmosphere in the dressing room could not have been better. The great respect which flowed between players and the Committee was highlighted by the brilliant partnership Evans enjoyed with Spencer. Both were young players yet the selectors and the rest of the team trusted the two 'Babes' to protect the goal as the last line of defence.

* * *

Which leads us on to probably the finest right-back of all time; the incredible Howard Spencer. The number '2' held magical connotations for Spencer, apart from the two medals he won in 1897. He, of course, made the number two shirt his own at Villa. He was also the possessor of two nicknames; 'The Prince of Full-Backs' and 'Gentle Howard'. Further, he possessed 'two good feet'

Howard Spencer

which he used to equally terrific effect. But he went one better than his lucky number by becoming the only Villa player to ever collect three FA Cup winners medals with the Club.

Brummie born and bred, Spencer attended Albert Road school in Aston, and never moved too far away from the Club he adored. He lived for many years in Frederick Road, a short walk across Aston Park from Villa's palatial home. Birchfield Trinity FC first took Howard out of the Albert Road school team, but in 1894 George Ramsay signed the man who would become a legend. He made his debut on 13th October of that year in a 3-1 home victory over the Albion and never looked back in a 42 year association with the club.

Another one of Villa's all-rounders, Spencer excelled at tennis, cricket and billiards. (In the latter, he might be able to dispute current Villa skipper Andy Townsend's unofficial title of Villa's green

baize king.) Amazingly enough, the Birmingham press circulated a rumour in 1896 that young Howard was contemplating retirement. Some mistake!

What a record of achievement Spencer attained with Aston Villa. FA Cup Winners in 1895, 1897 and then again as skipper in 1905. Then there were the League titles of 1894, 1896, 1897, 1899 and 1900. Between 1897 and 1905 he won a criminally low six caps for England including two coveted appearances against Scotland.

His first two seasons with the Club saw him score his only two goals in first-class football. Then came the great year on which we are reflecting. The following season (1897/8) Howard suffered an injury early on. That loss after just six games surely contributed to the 'mediocrity' of a year in which the Club finished 6th in the League and suffered 1st Round defeat in the Cup. His first benefit match in 1900 was the prelude to another injury which wiped out the 1901/2 campaign for Spencer though, thankfully, not his career. The 1904/5 season saw his form dip dramatically and he was dropped. Most fans and pundits believed Spencer was past it but injuries, this time to other players, gave him his chance and he proved his critics wrong. Coming back better than ever, he skippered his side to Cup triumph over Newcastle and then captained England against both Wales and Scotland to end an incredible year. A further benefit was granted in 1906 before he retired a year later having achieved everything a footballer could achieve.

After such a fruitful career, it is hard to imagine that Spencer had his detractors, but he did. The press bemoaned his *"weak kicking"* and the 'Gentle Howard' tag was not always a term of affection from the crowd who, predictably, loved the 'hard nut'. But Howard relied on brain not brawn. His tackling was supreme and he read the game so well that his anticipation - likened to that possessed today by Paul McGrath - meant he was always in the right place at the right time.

Spencer himself showed how far ahead of their time the Villa were through his attitude and belief about the art of full-back play. Writing in the 1905 *Book Of Football* he claimed to dislike backs who wellie the ball upfield, preferring instead to clear to an area where the forwards had a chance of picking up the ball and turning defence into attack: *"The man who puts the ball further than his forwards is merely giving a back on the other side a chance of doing something better than he himself has just done."*

As for claims that he didn't 'put himself about' enough, Spencer frowned upon foul play and believed that cheats never prospered: " *...you* *should learn to play with your head in a dual sense. Above all, believe me, there is nothing to be gained by unfair play. I have always believed that it is possible to get the best results by straight-forward, honest, and honourable football. Even supposing that once in a way you do, by a little mean trick, gain an advantage, surely the time comes when you attempt something illegal, and so give away a penalty which will probably carry with it a goal."*

The fact of the matter is that Spencer didn't need to bundle opponents because he was too good for them. Even if a forward got the better of him, his powers of recovery were so great that before the opposition could take advantage, Spencer was back up and had whipped the ball away. Yet not everyone appreciated this. Even the International selectors prevented him from being the regular England right-back - a position no other could fill as well - because they didn't think him strong enough.

One should not, however, read too much into the 'Gentle Howard' tag. John Devey - also writing in the *Book Of Football* - said: *"I often used to try and get Spencer fully roused* (with harsh words), *because he never plays so magnificently as when he is on his mettle. I always liked to see opponents ruffle Howard just a little. It takes a great deal to even ruffle him slightly, but when ruffled just a little he used to play his greatest game."*

Judging by the sustained level of excellence he displayed during his career, Spencer must have been permanently ruffled. That said, having heard Spencer's beliefs about the game, it is not difficult to justify the oft repeated turn of the Century comment which stated that Aston Villa typified all that was best in English football, and Howard Spencer all that was best in Aston Villa. It was a sad day when, after nearly 300 appearances, he became the last of the great Double winning team to leave the Club's playing staff.

He was not, though, lost to the Club. In 1909 he was elected to the Board on which he served alongside, amongst others, John Devey, George Ramsay and Frederick Rinder. Perhaps his greatest act as a director came in 1927 when he accompanied John Devey on a scouting trip to Tranmere. Their message to the Board upon their return was a simple one: *"Buy 'Pongo' Waring!"* In 1936, his official association with the Villa ended when he resigned his directorship. It was a time of mixed emotions. On the one hand, the Club had just been relegated for the first time in their history; a fate the whole world thought could never befall the great Aston Villa. However, in a great selfless act so typical of the man Peter Morris called: *"The greatest Villa great of them all..."* Spencer stood down to accommodate the return of Frederick Rinder who would again regenerate the Giant.

Spencer died at his Four Oaks home in the beginning of 1940. A very wealthy man, he had used his earnings from his playing days to build up the hugely successful 'Spencer Abbot Fuel Merchants' business. A true gentleman in every sense of the word, Howard lived his life following a simple tenet which he himself described: *"All that a man can try to do is let his side down as seldom as he can. He cannot hope to be immaculate."*

Some may disagree To those who saw the quietly spoken man with a penchant for fine cigars give his regular demonstrations of the full-back art, he was at his worst at least as good as any other player, and at his best he surpassed perfection - if such a thing is possible.

No one in the entire history of Aston Villa Football Club, from 1874 to the present day, could justifiably claim to be more committed to the Club than Howard Spencer. Loyal and vocal fan, player of legendary brilliance, inspirational skipper and genuinely benevolent director. Spencer himself would be too modest to accept such praise and would never seek personal accolades, although he surely deserves them more than any other.

He may have been the 'Prince of Full-Backs' and could probably (if anyone could) lay claim to a title of 'Mr. Aston Villa'. But what is beyond doubt is that, as a permanent fixture during the greatest period of one-club domination the world would see at least until the 1980's and perhaps ever, Spencer was the 'King of Footballing Excellence'. To all proud Villa fans, Gentle Howard is the man who embodies all that is good about the Club, yet at the same time is not in the slightest bit tarnished with that which is bad.

Chapter Three

Autumn Gold

Before Villa travelled to Derby to continue their League programme, there was good news for Howard Spencer. He had been picked to represent the Football League against the League of Ireland in Belfast in November. Not such glad tidings emanated from the Reserve team. In '95/6, they had won the Birmingham and District League title but this time round they were struggling. On 17th October, while the first team were performing extremely well at the Baseball Ground, the second-stringers could only manage a home draw with Redditch Town.

On a day when nearly 70,000 spectators watched the eight first division matches, 8,500 witnessed Villa jump to fourth in the League with a win against a strong Derby County side. The home team had been scoring freely on their own patch - although they'd been conceding a few as well and would have been much higher than 12th but for their inability to score in their first two away matches.

A possible reason for Villa's slow start and their failure to string two consecutive wins together was that they had yet to field the same line-up in successive matches. At Derby, stability was finally gained with the following eleven taking the field as they had done a week earlier to defeat West Brom:

Whitehouse, Spencer, Welford, Reynolds, Jas Cowan, Crabtree, Athersmith, Devey, Campbell, Wheldon, John Cowan.

The game was played at an exceptionally high pace from the start and both sides won corners within the first couple of minutes. The Villa forwards were showing their customary perfect combination but Derby made some dangerous speedy breaks which kept Whitehouse and his backs on their toes. Villa made a breakthrough on 9 minutes when Wheldon beat Robinson with a cleverly chipped shot. Sadly, this was ruled out thanks to a highly dubious offside decision and the scoresheet remained blank.

But the Villa continued to press. Three minutes later Campbell forced an amazing save from Robinson which proved the catalyst for a spell of pressure by the home side. The Derby forwards, though, found Whitehouse and especially Welford in fine form.

The latter, whilst steadfastly defending, set up a marvellous counterattack in the 24th minute. A brilliant tackle came in from Welford on the halfway line and he immediately laid a short pass to Crabtree. As John Cowan set off down the left wing, Crabtree shaped to play to the winger but instead sent a lovely disguised ball to Wheldon in the inside-left channel. Two Derby backs came to challenge the Villa forward who, with a dip of the shoulder, sent the duo the wrong way and strode elegantly towards the goal. With little back-lift, he hit a hard low shot, but Robinson looked to have it covered. That was until the intervention of Goodall who lashed out at the ball but only succeeded in diverting it into the net.

The score was credited to Wheldon, although nowadays video evidence would be used to confirm an own-goal. But, having had one perfectly legal strike ruled out, and after the skill he showed to shake off two defenders, no one could begrudge Fred his bit of luck. Anyway, the unfortunate Goodall didn't appear to want to take much credit for the score.

It took Derby 10 minutes to get back on level terms via a free-kick. The game was fast and clean, pleasing the crowd who were in fine voice throughout. The two custodians were often the beneficiaries of rousing ovations as they produced their best efforts to keep the sides level up to the interval.

The oranges having been munched, Villa came out strongly and Robinson was called upon to save his side on four occasions in the opening few minutes. Derby countered menacingly but lacked finish. At the other end, meanwhile, Athersmith suffered a 'Wheldon' when he too had a goal fall victim to a - this time justified - offside flag.

On the hour, though, a great move saw Wheldon find Campbell with a pinpoint pass. The Scottish centre side footed the ball home neatly to set the Brummie section of the crowd roaring.

Derby threw themselves forward to try and get back on terms but this just left them open to a quick break. It is always dangerous to adopt a 'gung-ho' approach against sides with speedy forwards and there was none faster than Charlie Athersmith. Derby discovered this when the outside-right broke out and, just when they thought he'd run out of pitch, Charlie delivered one of his stunningly accurate crosses. John Cowan, who had done well just to keep up with his teammate, calmly stroked the ball past Robinson to complete the scoring.

The goal knocked the stuffing out of County and, for the rest of the game, Villa stroked the ball around playing pure exhibition football. Two successive wins and, more importantly, commanding performances showed that last season's Champs were back in business. The forwards were majestic and, for the first time in the campaign, added accuracy to their shooting. But for the brilliance of Robinson in the home goal, double figures would not have been beyond Villa. Wheldon had some great runs and was well supported by John Cowan. Campbell dropped deep and brought the flanks into the game with some excellent passing. But it was the right-wing which killed Derby. Athersmith and Devey were in the kind of form that rendered them unstoppable. The half-backs were little short of perfect and the lastline, particularly Welford, dispirited the County forwards. This was Villa at their best.

They weren't anywhere near their best two days later when they went to Stoney Lane to begin the defence of the Staffordshire Cup. It had been announced that the full League team would play but Welford, Reynolds and Devey were rested, the latter's absence seriously affecting the effectiveness of the forwards. Evans, Burton and Chatt came in. The crowd of 5,000 saw Albion take a two goal lead before a Wheldon header from an Athersmith cross gave Villa a consolation strike.

There was a return to the line-up which had performed so well in the League, when Derby came to Perry Barr on 24th October. The visitors had changed their team thus fielding their strongest eleven. As would become a feature of the season, the confidence Villa evinced on their travels was replaced by a hesitancy, especially in front of goal, at Perry Barr. Despite having the advantage of the wind at their backs, Villa could not break down Derby's defence in an evenly matched goal-less first half.

Heavy rain throughout the second half caused much discomfort amongst the 10,000 crowd and the wind, which grew stronger as the game went on, played havoc with the Villa's passing game. Both 'keepers acquitted themselves well early on, but it was Robinson who was the first to have to scoop the ball out of the net. Athersmith had crossed to the head of John Cowan who directed the ball into the far corner.

Ten minutes later Athersmith was again the architect of Derby's downfall. He appeared to shape to cross but laid a lovely reverse pass along the deck to Campbell who guided the ball through to the onrushing Wheldon. He made no mistake. Although the Cradley Heath born great, Steve Bloomer, pulled one back for Derby, Villa had completed the double over the East Midlanders.

Athersmith tore his opponents to pieces throughout. At one point, it is said, he carried the ball past no less than eight players before messing up the easy bit by firing wide from six yards out. Wheldon too missed a sitter. At the other end, the agile Whitehouse brilliantly denied both Stephenson and Bloomer during a spell of sustained Derby pressure. But, despite John Cowan playing most of the second half carrying an injury, it was the Villa forwards who stole the show. The crocked winger was nursed through by Crabtree, the best half-back on the field.

* * *

Despite having put together a stronger squad than any of their rivals, the Villa Committee were always on the lookout for talent which could strengthen their hand still further. The latest player to catch George Ramsay's eye was Francis Beckton, the exciting Liverpool forward. The Villa had tried to buy him when he was at Preston but were pipped by the Merseysiders. No doubt Beckton reached that decision because he knew that a move to Villa carried with it the unenviable prospect of having to depose John Devey if he were to enjoy regular first-team action at Perry Barr.

So Villa, minus Beckton despite intense press speculation, took a large following to Stoke on 31st October. The travelling support was as welcome to the home Club as they were to the 'Pets'; the crowd only just exceeded 6,000 and a good proportion had come on the London and North West Railway Company's cheap half-day excursion from Birmingham.

On the pitch, changes were forced on the selectors by the injury John Cowan sustained a week earlier and Crabtree's unavailability due to a leg strain. Frank Burton regained the left-half spot while, in front of him, Steve Smith lined-up on the wing for his first appearance of the season. Smith's early-season absence from the team highlighted the depth of the squad. There weren't many sides who could afford to leave an International in the reserves.

In the first half Villa outplayed Stoke but only had one strike from the majestic Wheldon to show for their efforts. Even on the soft ground, the visitors' passing was fast and accurate, but the poor state of the playing surface around the goal mouths caused no end of problems. Twice Devey and once Campbell found themselves planted on their backsides after slipping when the goal was at their mercy.

For half an hour of the second period Stoke's bustling tactics gave them the upper hand. Villa didn't help their cause by neglecting Athersmith in favour of feeding Smith who was not playing well. His poor form did not, however, prevent him from notching a second goal as Villa ended the game the stronger.

In the final fifteen minutes, Athersmith did receive good service and murdered the Stoke backs with his pace. Wheldon too caused no end of problems with his fine dribbling. Three times he hit the woodwork and twice had goals disallowed for offside.

In the period that Stoke had the upper hand they found Spencer and Welford in their best form. Whitehouse, meanwhile, did everything that was asked of him. A fine day was capped with news that the reserves had beaten Small Heath 4-2 at Perry Barr, although the second team were still only averaging a point a game in the Birmingham and District League.

October had ended with a fourth consecutive win. Five matches unbeaten had seen Villa score nine goals and concede only two in the course of taking nine points from a possible ten. Sitting nicely in third place just one point behind the leaders, Bolton, the 'Pets' had identical home and away records. The press were now talking about the Championship. They argued that only Villa themselves could conspire to prevent the glorious trophy from extending its stay in Brum by a further twelve months.

* * *

Away from the immediate priority of securing League points, work at the Aston Lower Grounds was moving on apace. So confident were the Board of completing the job by Easter 1897, they approached the FA to ask for that year's England vs. Scotland international to be played at the stadium. The bid failed and the match took place at Crystal Palace, but two years later Villa Park was chosen as the venue for that most prestigious match.

Until the grand new home was ready for occupation, Wellington Road would continue to play host to Villa matches like the one against Bury on 7th November. Villa's lowest home crowd of the season (5,000) made their way to Perry Barr, most of them discussing the news that Villa had again

dipped into the transfer market. It turned out that they hadn't, but the alleged signing of Albion Rovers left-back, Peter Boyle, showed how far over the top newspaper speculation was a century ago. The Scottish Referee announced the 'transfer that never was' and went on to list contract terms and fees in incredible detail. Boyle, who had also attracted interest from Sunderland and Third Lanark, had cost Villa £50. He had been paid a £10 signing-on fee and would enjoy a weekly wage of £2.10s. Or not. He never played for Villa, indeed he never came to Villa.

He certainly wasn't in the line-up which faced Bury. Neither were Burton and Spencer. The former made way for a recovered James Crabtree while Albert Evans surprisingly replaced the injured Spencer. In the past, Howard's absences saw Crabtree partner Welford at the back and Burton filling in at left-half. In this instance however, the Committee decided to hand Evans his Villa debut.

Heavy rain had not only lowered the attendance but also levelled the teams. To paraphrase the Birmingham Daily Post, Bury played with dash which proved rather more effective than the passing game which Aston Villa stubbornly stick to. Yes, the press were still on at Devey's boys to 'hoof' the ball, asking: "Why will they not accommodate themselves to the state of the ground?"

They had a point actually. Villa had the lion's share of possession but, in attempting to be too clever, often found themselves slipping and sliding or simply being bundled off the ball. Things started well with Athersmith scoring his first goal of the season with a fine long-range effort. But, in a game when the backs on both sides held the upper hand, it was the only meaningful shot a claret and blue shirted player attempted all day. The Villa would have had both points too, but for an error by the otherwise faultless Welford. He misjudged a Plant cross and Miller levelled. Final score 1-1.

There is precious little good to say about an atrocious game which perfectly matched the conditions. It again served to prove something successive generations of Villa fans have known: Villa can demolish the top teams but just cannot play well against the bottom clubs. Bury were in last place going into the match and, even in a Double winning year, Villa showed their traditional abysmal form against a very poor side.

Rather than leave the game on such a depressing note though, the quote of the season appeared in the Birmingham Daily Post's match report. Talking about Fred Wheldon, they commented: "We expected him to play better than he did for he had a good apprenticeship in the mud at

Small Heath." No wonder the Small Heath Committee were always complaining about their press coverage!

* * *

Messrs. Cook & Son spotted the money which could be made by transporting Villa fans round the country. Thus they offered cheap packages for supporters wishing to follow the side to the Olive Grove ground of Sheffield Wednesday on 14th November. Wednesday had a home record on a par with fourth place Villa's but the visitors boasted the best away figures in the League. The *Birmingham Daily Post* noted the success Villa were having on their travels and commented that this was pleasing the rail companies who were coining it in from Villa's travelling support. Nearly a thousand of the faithful were contained within the 8,000 who attended the match.

They didn't have long to wait for a goal. Two minutes to be precise. Villa, attacking from the off, won a free kick. Bob Chatt (who had come in due to Reynolds being ill) floated the ball towards the head of Wheldon who easily found the net. The goal stung Wednesday into life and up to the interval they pushed forward menacingly but always looked like being caught out as Villa counter-attacked well.

The second half began at a tremendous pace. Devey was put through but shot straight at Massey. Wednesday came back and pressed down on Villa until eventually, and despite the best efforts of Welford and a recovered Spencer, they wore the visitors down. Whitehouse did well to palm out a free-kick but could do nothing to stop Brash following up.

On 70 minutes Villa were back in front. Campbell carried the ball three-quarters of the length of the field before a deft back-heel found Wheldon. He dodged a defender only to find his path to goal blocked so he stroked a return pass to Campbell who placed the ball into the net. Allegedly, even the home supporters cheered what was a truly magnificent goal.

The Villa were now rampaging through the Wednesday defence. Great work down the left by Smith and Wheldon spread panic through the home team's backs. Smith got away from his marker and crossed. Athersmith read the flight of the ball perfectly and nipped in to poke home Villa's third and make the final result the same as in the previous season's encounter.

It was a particularly welcome strike for Charlie who had, in the first half, lashed out in temper following a heavy challenge by Langley. Obviously rattled, Athersmith's game had suffered as a con-

sequence. He was better after the interval but, for a change, Smith and Wheldon on the left outshone the right-wing throughout the match. The Langley - Athersmith bout was typical of the nasty challenges which marred the game. The referee failed to keep order and foul play by each side went unpunished while the game was persistently halted for the more innocuous challenges.

But on a positive note, Welford gave one of his best performances of the season and Smith was playing well enough to suggest that John Cowan, who had recovered from injury but was now out through illness, would not get back into the first eleven for some time. Meanwhile, the *Birmingham Daily Post* had this to say about an awesome half-back: *"Crabtree showed the crowd to what pitch of perfection a footballer can attain."*

Following the Olive Grove victory, confidence was high when, a week later, Wednesday paid a visit to Perry Barr for the return match. For a change, that confidence was in no way misplaced. Villa had performed much better on their travels than they had before their home supporters but on 21st November they showed Birmingham the kind of form that their away following had come to expect.

In the first 45 minutes, there was not a great deal to choose between the two sides. Villa had easily the majority of possession and, as usual, looked the more polished outfit. But Wednesday broke away on a number of occasions and caused a few scares in the home defence. For their part Villa, playing downhill, used their incredible skills to get into excellent positions only to see a return of the poor shooting which had dogged their opening games. This, more than anything else, contributed to the 0-0 half-time scoreline.

The second half was entirely different. No defence could have dealt with the Villa forwards who suddenly hit heights which most teams could only dream of attaining.

Five minutes after the break, Athersmith went on a long run leaving numerous Owls in his wake. His cross was met spectacularly on the volley by Wheldon but Massey produced a miracle save to protect his charge. Soon after, a throw-in found Smith two yards out and he lashed the ball into the net with vicious force. The goal lifted Villa to new heights and they attacked the unfortunate Yorkshiremen incessantly.

Jas Cowan saw a ferocious long shot just go wide before Wheldon brought another spectacular save from Massey. Then Campbell went on an astonishing fifty yard run, supported all the way by Athersmith. Having broken through the Sheffield rear-guard, Campbell drew Massey and knocked the ball sideways for Athersmith to run it into the empty net. Soon after, Smith thumped in a beauty of a cross which Devey coolly controlled before picking his spot with perfection.

Wednesday tried desperately to get something from the game. Brandon hit the bar and Whitehouse brilliantly denied Bell. It was, though, the only time the Villa custodian was called into serious action.

Near the end, Athersmith raced away and his cross dropped on the head of leading scorer Wheldon who notched his seventh first-class strike of the campaign and gave Villa their biggest win of the season so far, by four goals to nil. All the forwards played out of their skins with Campbell having his best game ever at the Wellington Road enclosure. The reason the forwards were so dominant, however, was the brilliant support they received from the half-backs. Chatt, Jas Cowan and Crabtree worked tirelessly and passed with precision throughout. The win took Villa into second place with only Bolton's slightly superior goal average keeping the Claret and Blue from the top-spot they had come to regard as theirs by right.

14,000 had seen Villa slaughter Wednesday, but only half that number paid to enter Ewood Park as Villa ended their November programme by visiting mid-table Blackburn Rovers who had suffered a 6-0 pasting at Derby the week before. This prompted their Committee to make major alterations in the team for the Villa match. The visitors had just one change with Albert Evans coming in for Welford at left-back.

Villa lost the toss and played into the wind in the first-half. From the kick-off, Athersmith raced away and centred to Wheldon. The inside-left saw his first shot saved by Joy and even though the ball rebounded to him, Fred's second shot met a similar fate to the first. Former Preston 'keeper Joy was kept busy all through the half whilst at the other end Whitehouse played the role of spectator. Any geographically ignorant passer-by stumbling upon the game would have sworn the Villa were the home team. Time and again the sweet passing of the Villa forwards tore through the Rovers' defence. The half-backs joined in too with Jas Cowan trying a few of his trade-mark long-shots.

Despite their dominance, Villa went into the break with just a one goal lead through a twenty yard John Devey cross-shot. As the teams resumed after the interval, Rovers - who had had no serious attack in the opening period - altered their front line. It seemed that the switch might work as Blackburn launched some menacing attacks only to be let down by poor shooting. That sounds familiar! But as the game wore on, Villa's greater strength told - a testament to the genius of

Joe Grierson.

Villa's second goal, had television cameras been around in those days, would have been shown again and again - and enjoyed star billing on those Danny Baker 'cock-up' videos. Devey sent in a low shot which Joy saved. Campbell raced in (remember this was in the days of 'charging the goalie') and Joy tried to dispose of the ball quickly. In his rush, with a swoop of his arm, the unfortunate 'keeper threw the ball straight into the net. 'Joy for Villa' suddenly had a dual meaning.

Shortly after that comic goal, Campbell sent in a violent long-range effort which Joy did well to palm away. Smith, ever alert to the half-chance, was following up and scored his third of the season and his side's third of the match. Blackburn, to their credit, kept going and a free-kick following a hand-ball was placed into the crowded goalmouth by Anderson. In the resulting melee, the ball was scrambled past Whitehouse for what turned out to be no more than a consolation for Rovers. They did not attack again. Devey and Campbell both tested Joy before Wheldon found the bottom right-hand corner with a lovely 88th minute snap-shot. Campbell then rounded off the rout on the call of time. If any player in this match deserved a goal it was John Campbell who had, until his last-gasp effort, appeared fated not to score.

In a perfect performance, Jas Cowan stood out as easily the best halfback on the field. Not altogether surprising as many considered him the best half-back in the world. The forwards combined magnificently and their passing was of an order which at that time, and perhaps even today, was higher than most could have imagined possible. Individual skill had been married to brilliant teamwork. Short quick passes, long yet accurate cross-field balls and a shoot on sight policy put an on-song Aston Villa head and shoulders above the rest. As if to prove this point, the humiliation of Blackburn sent Villa to the top of the table for the first time this season. The rest of the League must have been dispirited at the sight of the following list:

			home				away					
	pld	w	d	l	f	a	w	d	l	f	a	g.av	pts
1 Aston Villa	14	4	2	1	14	7	5	1	1	17	8	2.07	21
2 Bolton	13	4	1	0	10	1	4	2	2	14	11	2.00	19
3 Liverpool	16	4	2	1	12	6	2	3	4	11	13	1.53	18
4 Preston	14	6	1	1	23	13	1	3	2	9	8	1.52	18
5 Sheff U	12	2	4	0	9	5	3	2	1	10	7	1.58	16
6 Derby	14	5	1	2	28	15	1	1	4	5	10	1.32	14
7 W Brom	14	4	2	3	7	6	1	2	2	5	8	0.86	14
8 N. Forest	13	4	2	1	17	8	0	3	3	5	12	1.10	13
9 Sheff W	13	4	1	2	15	10	1	2	3	6	13	0.91	13
10 Blackburn	14	4	1	3	11	13	1	2	3	3	14	0.52	13
11 Everton	12	3	1	3	15	10	2	1	2	5	7	1.18	12
12 Bury	13	2	3	1	11	9	1	3	3	6	13	0.77	12
13 Stoke	14	3	1	2	5	5	1	1	4	9	10	0.93	9
14 Wolves	12	2	1	3	5	5	1	1	4	9	10	0.93	8
15 Burnley	13	2	3	1	8	7	0	0	7	8	24	0.52	7
16 Sunderland	13	1	1	2	5	8	1	2	6	6	16	0.46	7

At the end of Chapter One, it was mentioned that Villa needed to string a few wins together. Oh how they responded to that challenge! Seven victories in nine matches unbeaten. Their 'goals for' column had been boosted by 22 at the expense of just 5 breaches of their own defence. That doesn't just represent Championship form, but is the sign of a team far, far ahead of its rivals. The key was undoubtedly the great form away from home. Their travelling record was the best in the League and would remain that way to the end of the season.

It wasn't all good news though. The fact that John Reynolds had not played in the last three games prompted reports that he had been suspended by the Committee for disciplinary reasons. This led George Ramsay to send the following communique to newspapers:

" Statements have been made that J. Reynolds has recently been guilty of misconduct. I am asked by the directors to say that such is not the case and that their relations with Reynolds during the whole of this season have been of a most friendly nature."

So there! The Reynolds case serves to highlight just what big news Villa were. Any little snippet of information was lapped up greedily by press and public alike. It was a similar story with the speculation surrounding the bid for Beckton, although at least there had been a fire behind that particular 'smoke'. Not any more though. Beckton, it was announced, was staying at Liverpool. It seems the Villa would just have to 'make do' with their current squad. One wonders if the Committee were worried by that prospect!

Chapter Four

Unsung Heroes
Half-backs

As the season entered the festive month, Aston Villa's forwards were at last finding their scoring boots The defence was as solid as ever and receiving well deserved praise. In between those two departments stood the backbone of the side: the half-backs. Solid in defence, enterprising in attack, the middle line was often overlooked by the pundits who were, not altogether surprisingly, drawn to the magic of the front-line and the coolness of the full-backs.

Six half-backs were used in season 1896/7 with only the centre-half rock, Jas Cowan, being ever-present. He, John 'Baldy' Reynolds and James Crabtree we shall come to, but first the reserves who were ever-ready to step into the breach.

Bob Chatt was the best known of the back-up squad. The second Barnard Castle born player at the Villa (Albert Evans being the other), Chatt joined the 'Pets' as a 22 year old in 1892. Prior to that, he had spent four highly successful seasons at Joe Grierson's Middlesbrough Ironopolis club, where he notched up a half century of goals. This alerted the Villa to the young star and, having paid a small fee to Ironopolis, they gave Chatt his debut in a 6-4 home win over Accrington.

Occasional appearances in '93/4 set Bob up for his most successful season of all. Having scored 12 goals in 28 appearances in the inside-right position during the 1894/5 campaign, Chatt lined up at Crystal Palace for the penultimate game of the year - the FA Cup Final. As we have already discovered, that match was settled with a goal after 30 seconds scored by John Devey. However, as so many record books list Chatt as the scorer, it is difficult to know whether to feel sorry for Devey, who has had such a great honour denied him by historians, or for Chatt whose place in history belongs to someone else.

The following year, Bob Chatt picked up a Championship medal although, now looked upon more as a forward than a half, his place had seemed under threat by the arrival of John Campbell. But Chatt managed 18 games, some at centre-half, some in the left-half position and a number at inside-right as Villa battled against injuries to key forwards, Smith and Hodgetts.

Bob Chatt

In the Double year (which was cut short for Chatt owing to a toe injury) and the subsequent campaign he added a further 30 games to his record before returning to the North-East - and making history. Following his departure from Villa, he was reinstated as an amateur and signed for Stockton with whom he won an Amateur Cup winners medal in 1899, making him one of a very select few to have won both FA and Amateur Cup gongs. His playing career ended with spells at South Shields and Willington Athletic before he was appointed trainer at Manchester City in 1906.

Bob Chatt died in 1935. For just one season he had held down a regular place at the greatest football club in the world. Yet in terms of medals won and magic moments experienced, he had surpassed the achievements of some of the game's immortals.

* * *

At around the same time Bob Chatt was bought, Frank Burton arrived at the Villa from Walsall Town. Initially, he made a bigger impression - and more appearances - than Chatt. But much of Villa's first championship season ('93/4) was wiped out for Burton thanks to the purchase of John Reynolds. That became the story of Frank's career - understudy. Injuries to Reynolds gave Burton his longest run in the team in the 1895/6 Championship season when he played in half Villa's games.

Frank Burton

He was a good player without ever setting the world alight. The press often slated him with the *Birmingham Daily Post* commenting during the Double season: *"He is simply not good enough for the League eleven."* Sadly for Frank, he was constantly compared with Crabtree and Reynolds - two players from a different class. After six years and 53 appearances at the Club, he retired from football.

* * *

The final 'back-up' half-back was Jeremiah Griffiths. Born in Brum in 1872, he was recruited from Birmingham St. George's and played just three games for Aston Villa; one in '95/6 and two in '96/7 - one against Bolton in the last first-team game to be played at Perry Barr, the other an FA Cup semi-final. With James Crabtree being called upon to cover when injuries hit the full-backs or forwards, the opportunities to enjoy League action in the half-back line were relatively numerous. But Griffiths found himself behind Chatt and Burton in the pecking order, and neither of those could hold their places when Reynolds, Cowan and Crabtree were available. So, in November 1897 he moved to Bilston Town before ending his career at Bloxwich Strollers.

* * *

The reason for the back-up halves' lack of first-team action was simple. Reynolds, Cowan and Crabtree were individually the best half-backs in the world and collectively, it could be argued, the

best half-back line of all time. It is possible that Villa could have lost a player from the front or back departments of the team and still won the Double. But taking one of the halves out for the season would have probably seen 1896/7 become just another year in the life of Aston Villa Football Club.

Of the three, John 'Baldy' Reynolds was the crowd's favourite. This was a little surprising as any Villa fans who travelled to The Oval on 19th March 1892 would have been cursing Reynolds and his ten West Brom comrades who soundly whipped Villa in the FA Cup Final. Reynolds scored the third goal in that match. A little over a year later and an incredibly low £40 transfer fee had been exchanged for 'Baldy'. Ironically, his Villa debut came at Perry Barr against Albion on the opening day of the 1893/4 campaign. Reynolds scored a penalty in Villa's 3-2 win!

John's story began in Blackburn where he was born in February 1869. He grew up in Ireland and this led to much confusion over his nationality, hence he played five times for Ireland (including all three Home Internationals in 1891) before being capped by England on eight occasions after his birthplace was revealed.

He returned to his home town at the age of fifteen and two years later joined the East Lancashire Regiment. His first posting was in... Ireland. Perhaps his nickname should have been yo-yo! Of course, he played Army football and,

John 'Baldy' Reynolds

having completed three years service, left the forces and was immediately signed by Distillery in 1889. A year later he joined Ulster and won his first Irish cap. In 1891 he gained an Irish Cup winners medal before West Bromwich Albion brought him back to England.

Having put Villa to the sword at The Oval, he came to Perry Barr and immediately won the crowd over. His prematurely receding hairline was the source of much good-hearted banter with the supporters.

The next four years saw him make 110 highly successful appearances for the Villa. In his first season, he picked up a Championship medal and scored seven of his 17 goals in claret and blue. The following year, he was the star of the Cup winning team. Then, a second title was won before the Double was completed in '96/7.

What a final season Reynolds enjoyed in Birmingham. Apart from the Double, he played for England against Scotland, a game in which he was easily his side's man of the match. A sign of how highly rated 'Baldy' was came with his five appearances in six years against the Auld Enemy. The Scots cap was the highest honour an English player could receive at the time.

But he decided not to re-sign for the '97/8 season. At first, their was speculation linking him with his home town club, Blackburn Rovers. In the end, he joined Jimmy Welford and John Campbell on a train to Glasgow where the three of them signed for Celtic in August 1897. In their first season north of the border, the Scottish Cup was won, thus making Reynolds the first player to play for English, Irish and Scottish cup winning teams.

Reynolds went on his travels towards the end of his career. He left Celtic for Southampton and then moved out to New Zealand where he spent a couple of years playing and coaching before returning to England in 1903 to play for Stockport County. That was followed by twelve months at Willesden Town before he retired in 1905 as Howard Spencer was leading the Villa to Cup glory. Having hung up his boots, John 'Baldy' Reynolds worked at a colliery near Sheffield until his death in March 1917. The right-half who combined solid defence with breathtaking dribbling was just 48 years old.

* * *

The *Birmingham Daily Post* said of James Crabtree: *"There is no better half-back in the world."* There also weren't too many better fullbacks nor, indeed, forwards. For the man who played in all five 'back' positions for England, whilst favouring the left-half berth, played in no less than seven positions for Aston Villa. His versatility was so great that his final season (1901/2) saw him alternate between the right and left-back slots without once moving up into the half-backs. During the Double year, he also made it into all three central forward positions. This prompted the *Daily Post* to comment: *" We wonder if we will ever*

see him in goal." He probably would have been world-class between the sticks too!

No single man maketh a team, but Crabtree was a entire team in himself. The secret behind his versatility was his footballing brain. He was a great thinker and master tactician. A student of half-back play, Jimmy could read a game so well that. wherever he found himself on the field of play, he could adapt to his surroundings. There was, quite simply, no other like him. Nowadays the value of utility players is recognised, but none of the modern day 'jacks of all trades' can match the quality Crabtree brought to every position he played.

James Crabtree

In was near Christmas 1871 that this exceptional footballer first arrived on Earth. His mission: To spread claret and blue joy where'er he roamed. This caused a certain confusion as, having been born in Burnley, it was his hometown claret and blue which first benefited from his services. Thankfully, that Club didn't realise what they had. Jimmy was farmed out to Rossendale and Heywood before returning to Burnley.

In July 1895, the Lancastrians thought they had got the mother of all deals when the Villa offered a 'ridiculous' record transfer fee of £250 for Crabtree. Burnley gratefully grabbed the cash and Villa... got an absolute bargain. The price tag caused such a storm that the public flooded into Perry Barr to see the man who had cost such an enormous amount, as the squad completed their pre-season training. Many of those who came to see stayed to buy season tickets. Today's football supremos, it seems, cannot hold a light to George Ramsay when it comes to acquiring players who will put bums on seats. The Villa man carried sound football and business sense with him during his forays into the transfer market.

The style of play Crabtree (the half-back) brought with him to Wellington Road, he himself described in 1905. Paraphrasing his words from the *Book of Football,* halves have to be fine tacklers, supreme passers who don't just play in a colleague but distribute the ball to the 'best placed' team mate, and they must possess a good eye for goal. What is more, they must do everything instinctively.

Crabtree could do these things (except score) better than anyone, with the possible exception of Jas Cowan and Ernest 'Nudger' Needham of Sheffield United. Even those two could never claim to be more than Jimmy's equal. And Crabtree's skills didn't end with the above list. He had incredible close-control which he used to great effect by dribbling through crowded midfields to take his team deep into enemy territory.

His first season with Villa saw him win the first of four Championship medals with the Club. His claret and blue (Mk.II) career saw him play exactly 200 games but, as has already been hinted at, he managed a poor seven goals at an average of one a season.

James W. Crabtree bade farewell to Aston Villa in May 1902 when he began the first of two spells at Oreston Rovers. Sandwiched in between was a spell at Plymouth Argyle. He won 14 caps and had the honour of playing in the first International match to be held at Villa Park. In 1896, 1899 and 1900, he completed the 'clean sweep' by appearing in all three Home Internationals.

After retiring in 1906, Crabtree (like so many men who have come into contact with the City of Birmingham and its premier football club) returned to the great Midlands metropolis. Another for whom the phrase 'Once a Villa man...' had especial significance. Crabtree died in June 1908. It was a sudden death which spirited away the 36 year old genius who took half-back play to unprecedented heights.

* * *

When Crabtree and Reynolds lined-up in the two wing-half positions, they had between them the greatest centre-half of the entire 'W' formation era: James Cowan. Known to one and all as Jas, he stood a mere 5' 6½" tall yet was an exceptional tackler, possessed a brilliant tactical mind, a fine turn of pace and, in the words of Albert Evans: *"...could shatter inside forwards on his own."*

17th October 1868 saw the birth of Jas in - appropriately enough - Jamestown, Scotland. He played for Vale of Leven Reserves despite the fact that his employer hated football and, if he'd known about Cowan's extracurricular activities, would

have immediately dismissed his employee. This ability to dupe his bosses would serve Jas well in one of the most famous tales from the annals of Aston Villa. But more about that later.

Jas Cowan

In 1889, Jas accepted an invitation from the Edgbaston based Warwick County club to come to Brum for a trial. This bit of news reached the ears of George Ramsay who set out to intercept his fellow Scot before County could get their mits on him. Sure enough, Ramsay got to his man before Jas had time to find his true destination. From that point on, it was a foregone conclusion that Cowan would become a Villa player, for Ramsay always got his man. Anyway, Jas wasn't allowed to leave Ramsay's sight until he had signed a League form for the Perry Barr Pets. In the lounge of the Old Crown & Cushion, the stoney-faced muscular centre-half joined the club he would make 354 appearances for in thirteen seasons.

When Cowan became the first of the Double winning side to join the Club, Aston Villa were on a downward spiral which required the forceful intervention of Frederick Rinder to halt and reverse. While changes were implemented behind the scenes, Jas remained the rock on which was built one of the best teams in history. In the Double year, he was ever-present for the fourth season since joining Villa.

It was indeed rare that Cowan failed to make the starting line-up. There was, however, a six game period between 7th December 1895 and January 4th 1896 when Jas did not play. The reason has gone down in Villa legend.

Jas needed some money, probably to pay for his wedding due to take place in the summer of 1896. Being blessed with a good turn of speed (though he was no sprinter) he decided he would have a good chance of winning the famous Powderhall Sprint - and the £80 first prize! The problem for Cowan was that he knew the Villa Committee would not allow him the time off to train and race.

The answer: The centre-half feigned a back injury. The Club had their star examined by a doctor who could find nothing wrong with the offending spine, but Jas's acting convinced everyone that there was a problem. The Club granted Cowan's request to return to Jamestown for rest and recuperation but insisted that the doctor accompany him. So it was that Cowan continued to act poorly when in the medical man's company - and went off running whenever the quack's back was turned.

On one occasion, Jas was nearly caught out when his training run took him close to where his 'minder' was staying, but the doctor - who was said to be short-sighted - couldn't be sure that the runner he saw was, indeed, his patient. Thus, on 2nd January 1896, Cowan lined-up at the start of the 130 yard race. He had entered under a pseudonym and been granted, wrongly as it turned out, a 12½ yard start. Cheering him on were Albert Evans, Bob Chatt and Charlie Athersmith, all of whom had put money on their friend at 6 to 1.

Jas won in a time of 12½ seconds, just holding out as the fools who had given him such a long start tried in vain to close him down in the last few yards. Cowan left the Edinburgh track with his wallet bulging, something Athersmith, Chatt and Evans could not say. As the trio went off to collect their winnings, the bookie who had taken their bet was doing a fine impression of Jas. He'd done a very speedy runner.

Of course, the winner of such a famous race was written about in every newspaper in the country. His 'bad back' was revealed as fraudulent and the Villa Committee were waiting for Cowan upon his return to Birmingham. They fined the player and slapped a four week ban on him. As was shown by Cowan's presence in the 1-0 home win over Preston on 11th January, however, the ban was lifted immediately. That was because even Fred Rinder - Villa's stern disciplinarian - saw the funny side of Cowan's escapade. Incidentally, Jas did put his winnings to good use when he was married on Wednesday 22nd July 1896.

So Jas could run. But what kind of footballer was he? His tackling has already been mentioned. Suffice to say he hit ball and man with equal force. He was truly a fearsome sight to opposing forwards and few were foolish enough to tangle with him. It was not until the legendary Frank Barson entered Villa Park that the Club could boast such a powerful centre-half.

But Cowan's game was not just physical. Quite the opposite in fact. By drumming in to Albert Evans the benefit of a well placed pass out of defence, Jas betrayed his obsession with keeping the ball on the deck. Were he alive today one thing is certain: he would not support Wimbledon. It was easy for Jas to extol the merits of accurate passing because he always made time for himself to pick out a colleague, even during periods of intense pressure. It was strange to see such a physical tackler crunch into an opposing forward and then lay a delicate ball to his own attackers. But that was Jas.

Strangely for one who liked ball to touch grass as often as possible, a regular feature of his game was the long shot which nearly always flew miles over the bar. So common was this sight that it earned the nickname: *"The Cowan Skyscraper"* amongst the Wellington Road faithful in whose affections Jas was second only to 'Baldy' Reynolds. People were naturally drawn to him for no apparent reason. He never 'played up' to the crowd nor was he a particularly outgoing character. He simply dominated every match he played in.

Off the pitch, Jas was a quiet figure. It took much effort to get him to loosen up. But, when he was forced out of his shell, his comrades often wished they'd left him alone. Every now and again, the Old Crown & Cushion would vibrate to the booming sound of Jas belting out traditional Scottish songs. And once in full voice, it was a brave man who tried to stop Cowan, just as it was a brave forward who invited a tackle from the iron man.

Just as 1896/7 represented the zenith of Aston Villa Football Club's achievements, so it was a tremendous campaign for Jas Cowan. Selected to play for Scotland against England at Crystal Palace, his no-nonsense tackling and pinpoint passing earned him the title man of the match in the eyes of all who witnessed the game. Indeed, the only player who came close to upstaging Jas was John Reynolds who lined up on the opposite side to his club-mate. A week later both players were back at the south London ground for a match in which, according to the *Birmingham Daily Post*, Jas was the best player amongst twenty-two greats. That game was the FA Cup Final.

In season 1901/2 Cowan played just one game. As his career wore on he neglected his training, put on weight and lost form. At the end of that season he took up the Committee's offer of a job coaching the Villa youth team. Jas hung up his boots having collected five Championship medals and played in three Cup Finals, two of which found him on the winning side. He could also proudly boast of having played more games for the world's greatest football club than any other (although this record was short-lived as Billy George overtook Cowan's mark later in that same decade). Perhaps the only shadow on a brilliant career was his amazingly low number of Scottish caps. Three years running he played against England but they were his only International appearances. This can be explained by the fact that the Scotland selectors rarely picked players from the English League. Their loss!

For four years, Villa's youngsters benefited from Cowan's guidance. Then he moved to the Capital to become Queen's Park Rangers' first manager; a post he held for seven years until 1913 when he left the game for good and returned to Jamestown. There, two months after his fiftieth birthday, this great Villa legend died.

* * *

Aston Villa have fielded many great half-back lines over the years. Pearson, Leake, Windmill. Ducat, Barson, Harrop. Gibson, Talbot, Tate. Massie, Allen, Iverson. Blanchflower, Moss, Dorsett. Crowther, Dugdale, Saward. All those players - individually and in combination - would have walked into most Championship winning sides from 1889 to the end of the 'W' era. Yet none of them could quite match the perfection which was Reynolds, Cowan, Crabtree. The greatest of all-time. No question!

Chapter Five

Festivities and Hiccups

Top of the League at last, the team took time out from competitive football on 30th November to play a benefit match for an Old Villan, William Dickson. He had joined the Villa in 1889 from Sunderland and went on to play in four of the five forward positions for the Midlands' colossus. After scoring 34 goals in 64 appearances he transferred to Stoke City in 1892. It was while playing for them in a 4-3 defeat at Sheffield Wednesday on 26th September 1896 that he suffered an injury which ended his career.

So Villa sent a strong side to the Victoria Ground to play for their old comrade. City were happy to take a 3-0 win from the game while Dickson received the proceeds from a 2,000 crowd and, at the end of the season, a coaching post at Stoke.

From that leisurely stroll in Staffordshire, Aston Villa made their way south for a mini-tour of London. The one absentee was Jas Cowan who travelled in the opposite direction to defend his Powderhall Sprint title. This time he had the Committee's permission but lacked the vocal support of his team-mates. No doubt his trio of supporters weren't prepared to be fleeced by the bookies a second time! Nor were the organisers about to be duped into giving Jas such a large start (only 9½ yards this time) and the Villa centre-half narrowly failed to carry off first prize two years running.

Back in the Capital, the Villa took on the Corinthians at West Kensington's Queen's Club. Usually crowds for matches involving the famous amateur side barely scraped four figures but the League Champions proved a big draw and 5,000 turned up to watch the match.

The home team enjoyed greater possession in the opening twenty minutes but the Villa forwards showed the better combination. Villa were soaking up the pressure and hitting their opponents on the break. This policy reaped rich rewards as the visitors took a 3-1 lead from the first half. Early in the second, the Corinthians were awarded a penalty following a foul. There was a long stoppage as the home team did not seem to know what was going on. It turned out that penalties were so rare in Corinthians matches that none of the team was

sure what they should do. Eventually though, the spot kick was stroked home.

Villa restored their two goal lead midway through the half but sustained pressure by their hosts saw the match finish in a four-all draw. The Corinthians fight back surprised the crowd who, to a man, thought Villa had secured victory with their fourth strike.

Two days later on 7th December, a similar sized crowd saw Villa visit the Plumstead home of Woolwich Arsenal. The game was a benefit for the widow of ex-Arsenal star, Powell, who had died a week earlier. Playing with a strong wind, Wheldon, a returned Jas Cowan and Devey scored in quick succession to give the Midlanders a three goal lead at the break. Haywood pulled one back in the second period but Villa's science proved too much for Arsenal and the game ended 3-1.

Elsewhere there was bad news on two fronts. As Villa cruised to victory in south London, so Bolton were doing the same with a 2-0 home defeat of Everton. This sent Wanderers back to the top of the table on goal average. Meanwhile, John Cowan and Griffiths were both sent to Manchester to seek treatment from football injury specialist, Mr. Whitehead. The medical man had his work cut out as seven other players were also in his care.

* * *

Saturday 12th December saw a return to League action. Turf Moor was the destination as Villa sought victory over bottom club Burnley. The weather was terrible making the already very heavy pitch extremely treacherous, but Mr. Armitt, the referee, decided the match should go ahead.

Villa won the toss and played with the wind and rain at their backs and immediately attacked. Crabtree, who had moved up to centre forward as John Campbell was absent owing to a heavy cold, squandered a couple of good chances early on. He was not alone in this respect with Jas Cowan, Wheldon and Steve Smith all missing decent scoring opportunities. This made it all the more infuriating when the home team scored a surprise goal.

That seemed to add urgency to the Villa's play

and within five minutes they had raced into a 2-1 lead. Then, after 35 minutes play, Mr. Armitt did what he should have done much earlier and called the game off. The weather had won and the game would have to be replayed at a later date. For the time the match was in progress, it was noticeable that the Villa had taken their hosts too lightly. They were content to stroll through the match and paid the price when they fell a goal behind. This added a touch of urgency to the visitors' play and Villa came back into the game with ease. But there was a lesson to be learnt in that no opposition should be regarded as a push-over. Sadly, that is something successive Villa teams have failed to comprehend.

Two days later the team travelled to Barbourne in deepest Worcestershire to begin the defence of the Birmingham Senior Cup against Berwick Rangers. This match coincided with news that Lozells-lad Billy Garraty had signed a League form for Villa. He was too late to share in the Double glory that was unfolding, but he did earn the title 'Villa Great' by scoring 111 times in an eleven season, 256 game claret and blue career. As for the Cup match, 1,500 supporters saw the 'Pets' cruise to a 7-1 victory.

A somewhat eventful day was rounded off with a Presentation Dinner and Smoking Concert in honour of John Devey. A large gathering packed the Old Royal in Temple Row as Mr. J. Dunkley presided over events. George Ramsay, James Lees and Howard Vaughton were among the guests who heard the Villa skipper's old friend, Olly Whateley deliver a highly eulogistic speech. He praised Devey's: *"...great, successful and unique skill as an athlete over the past thirteen years, six of which have been spent connected with Aston Villa. As captain, John has kept up the fine tradition laid down by the great Archie Hunter."* In response, Devey - who never liked having to deliver speeches - said: *"My best services will continue to be given to the Villa club."* How true that comment turned out to be!

The Old Royal having been drunk dry, the team had five days to recover before the 19th December visit from Nottingham Forest. By covering the Wellington Road pitch with sand, the Villa ensured the game went ahead although the ground was very hard. The bitterly cold weather kept the crowd down to 7,000 as Forest came in search of their first away win of the season in their eighth excursion from Nottingham. For the Villa's part, three weeks on from their last (completed) League match, it was good to get back to competitive action.

The absence of John Campbell called for a fair bit of re-arrangement in the team. Crabtree moved up to centre forward and John Reynolds took the left-half berth with Bob Chatt continuing to occupy the opposite wing. The team lined up thus:

Whitehouse, Spencer, Evans, Chatt, Jas Cowan, Reynolds, Athersmith, Devey, Crabtree, Wheldon, Smith.

Forest kicked off and immediately won a free-kick. From this, there was a scramble in the home goal mouth and the ball was eventually cleared off the line by Evans. This set the pattern of the game with both sides going at each other at a terrific pace.

After 5 minutes play, Evans picked out Reynolds with a free-kick and his fast low shot put Villa ahead. Within a minute, the scores were level thanks to a Richards strike for the visitors. Then, another Evans set-piece found the head of John Devey who, in turn, hit the net. Only a quarter of an hour had been played. For the rest of the half, although Forest had their moments, it was Allsop in the visitors' goal who was the busiest man on the park. He was on great form too, with one fingertip save from the excellent Fred Wheldon bringing gasps of admiration from the crowd.

Within four minutes of the re-start, Villa had taken a 3-1 lead. The goal resulted from a cross-field ball of such precision that, in those days, it could only have come from a claret and blue man. Steve Smith was the genius who whipped the ball out to Charlie Athersmith on the other wing. The Villa's speed merchant then side-stepped Iremonger and unleashed a thunderbolt which, had Allsop got a touch on it would have taken the 'keeper into the net as well. A stunning goal had the crowd in raptures.

The Villa kept pressing but they were thwarted by brilliant goalkeeping. Yet it was Forest who eventually scored. A fast breakaway by the visitors resulted in a corner. From that, the ball beat Whitehouse but, having consulted the linesman, the referee ruled the 'goal' out because it had gone directly in. Nowadays of course - and as Steve Staunton can testify - the strike would have counted.

In the last fifteen minutes, Villa tired and Forest penned their hosts in their own half. Another corner resulted in a legitimate goal for Frank Foreman which reduced the deficit to one but Villa held out - just. The long gap between League matches had obviously told on the home team who lacked their usual fitness. No doubt Joe Grierson had them putting in more work on the training ground after that.

Villa also missed John Campbell whose precision passing was used to great effect in bringing the wingers into play. Crabtree was the best choice to replace the Scot as the alternative would be to upset the right wing by pulling Devey into the centre. But taking Crabtree from the left-half berth did not help the left-wing fire on all cylinders as he had built up a good understanding with Evans and Smith. Reynolds, however, did a good emergency job; he along with Whitehouse and the two full-backs shone throughout the match which also saw a return of the cross-field passes which were used to such great effect in '95/6. This prompted praise from the press who noted that Villa were showing signs of adapting their style to different playing conditions.

The win over Forest placed Villa back on top of the League as Bolton could only draw at home to West Brom. Villa would hold that position right to the end of the season.

Today's footballers often complain of over-work. One wonders how they would feel about having to spend Christmas Day playing a top of the table clash at Anfield. That is what the Villa players did in 1896. Interestingly, the Christmas Eve edition of the *Birmingham Daily Post* published the times of the trains on which the Villa team would be travelling, something which would certainly not happen today. It is a good example of how much closer to their fans football clubs were a hundred years ago.

Liverpool paid Villa £50 for playing the game on 25th December. On a lovely day, 25,000 fans packed the ground, all no doubt killing time while the turkey roasted. The home team had prepared for the game at Freshfield during the preceding week and, being only three points adrift of Villa going into the game, were looking to continue their own push for honours. It was never going to be easy for the Champions at Anfield as Liverpool had only conceded three goals in eight home matches since their return to the top flight.

Liverpool won the toss and kicked off. The game got off to a blistering start with both 'keepers tested early on. Beckton (remember him?) rounded Spencer and shot. A goal seemed the inevitable outcome but Crabtree (who had replaced the injured Albert Evans) raced back and hooked the ball out before it crossed the goal-line. Eight minutes in though, Beckton found the net after controlling a McVean cross.

Villa pressed, particularly through Athersmith down the right who was fed well by the recovered John Campbell, but this left them open to Liverpool's speedy breaks. One of these resulted in a shot which Whitehouse could only parry and Allan was on hand to double the Reds' lead. Straight from the restart, however, a Villa attack was checked but the ball fell to the feet of Jas Cowan nearly thirty yards out. This time there was

no 'skyscraper' as he blasted a shot into the corner of the net.

Villa were now well on top and five minutes after Jas had scored, Wheldon levelled matters from a couple of yards out. Liverpool were defending for their lives with Storer in goal being bombarded with shots which he did well to keep out. The home team were not used to being under the cosh on their home patch, but they hadn't faced the Villa there in '96! Despite Smith and Athersmith having brilliant games on the flanks, no further score was recorded in the opening half.

Two minutes into the second half, Spencer slipped leaving Michael with goal at his mercy. He placed his shot well but Whitehouse stretched his frame to the limit to pluck the ball out of the air in what was, in all likelihood, the save of the season.

The heavy ground began to take its toll on the players and the pace, which had been electric in the opening period, dropped markedly. The game had become a midfield battle with neither side able to get the upper hand. Liverpool finally managed to push Villa back. A shot following a corner headed towards the goal only to be punched out by one of the backs. It is not known exactly who handled the ball - the only certainty being that Howard Spencer did NOT do it because, well, he wouldn't cheat! Beckton (who else?) scored the penalty leaving the home supporters happy. They didn't stay smiling for long, however, as Villa kept working and were rewarded when Athersmith crashed the ball past Storer from twelve yards out to leave the final score at 3-3.

It was a great game played at an amazing pace for nearly an hour. Despite the extremely shoddy state of the pitch, both teams attacked with style and the Liverpudlian crowd were treated to a level of entertainment far greater than the Christmas TV schedules which their modern day counterparts must make do with.

Elsewhere that Christmas Day 1896, Derby County welcomed West Bromwich Albion, although perhaps 'welcomed' isn't quite the right word. County slaughtered their guests 8-1, the biggest win of the season by any team. The result meant that Derby had scored more goals at home in the first half of the season than any other side in the League had totalled from their home AND away matches!

* * *

The Villa left Liverpool on Boxing Day and almost got home to Birmingham. They made it as far as Wolverhampton where they were forced to stop at Molineux. Before the players could belatedly join in the festive spirit, they had to play a

League match against Wolves.

A heavy downpour in the morning had apparently adversely affected the size of the crowd. That said, 18,000 saw Villa start the game strongly. In the opening five minutes, Wheldon found himself well-placed on no less than three occasions, only to shoot straight at Tennant each time. The Wolves backs and halves were bemused by the skill and combination of the Villa forwards and could not break out of defence. The inevitable breakthrough came when Reynolds swung a free-kick into a crowded goalmouth. Chatt shot and the ball deflected off Owen into the net, although with or without Owen's intervention it was always going in.

The goal woke Wolves from their slumber and they immediately went on the offensive. Tonks rounded Crabtree and sent the ball to Miller but he missed when it would have been easier to score.

Villa stepped up their game and again pegged Wolves back. The visiting forwards were getting plenty of target practice. Devey hit the post and Campbell struck the crossbar as Wood and Owen at the back for Wolves were torn apart. Athersmith and Devey were on fine form despite the pitch being in such a bad state that often the ball would stop dead in the mud. But, defying the conditions, a typical Devey and Athersmith passing routine ended with the latter scoring his sixth goal in seven games to make it 2-0. The right-wing pair were assisted by the incredible work rate of Reynolds behind them. After playing on the left in the win over Forest, 'Baldy' had swapped sides with Chatt for the game at Anfield and remained in his favoured righthalf position at Molineux.

The Villa had been outplaying Wolves with ease and the crowd braced themselves for the expected goal rush. The home team, though, had other ideas and gradually pulled themselves back into the game. A free-kick was won in a dangerous position on the right. Malpas nipped in to meet the centre and pull a goal back for Wolves.

Still Villa had the better of things and, but for Tennant, double figures would have been a distinct possibility. Smith, Wheldon and Athersmith all brought the best out of the Wolves custodian. Meanwhile, on the stroke of half-time, Miller again squandered a golden opportunity during a rare Wanderers attack.

It was more even in the second half with the Villa defence having to work harder than in the opening period. Spencer and Crabtree, especially, played a grand game. Near the end, Smith of Wolves fell theatrically to the ground and claimed Spencer had illegally charged him. The referee waved away the home side's penalty claims and was resultantly faced with heavy criticism from the Black Country supporters. As everyone knows, however, Howard would not foul an opponent and certainly not in a position where he might give away a spot-kick!

There was no further score and the Villa had extended their unbeaten run to twelve games, only three of which had been drawn. Clear at the top of the table - when they had only been third at the same stage of their successful '95/6 campaign - everything was running along perfectly. This prompted the *Birmingham Daily Post* to end 1896 singing the side's praises:

"There can be no doubt now that the Villa are the finest combination in the country and we question if any club in the kingdom could hold them on a neutral ground. It is doubtful if they have ever been stronger and, given a little good fortune in the English Cup draws, they might this season succeed in bringing off the Double event."

* * *

The players finally got to swap presents with their families during the evening of 26th December having had a productive, if hard-working, Christmas. Meanwhile, their West Brom counterparts were showing perhaps too much good will to all men. Having let in eight at Derby, they plugged a couple of leaks at the back during the Black Country derby at Molineux on the 28th. This time they only lost 6-1. Well, it's an improvement!

Villa were back in action on the 29th, taking on Small Heath in front of a 5,000 crowd at Perry Barr. The game was a benefit for Villa full-back James Elliott who had not played for over a year owing to an illness which, it was now conceded, had ended his career. Athersmith was rested meaning a rare chance for reserve outside-right Field to play alongside the Club's star names. The 'keepers were the stars in an evenly-contested game. Villa were evidently treating the match as nothing more than a training session and the more committed Small Heath side took the lead after 35 minutes. The second half saw Villa encamped in the visitors half and, after some wayward shooting and a criminal miss by Wheldon, Smith headed home John Devey's cross to level the score.

* * *

A new year. The same awesome Villa line-up. But the signs were not good for 1897. The first problem was the *Birmingham Daily Post's* eulogy following the match at Wolves. It is no secret that once a team begin to be praised they falter and newspaper columnists were the Victorian equivalent of the 'Murray Walker Effect'. But the worst omen of all for Villa fans who had, more than once, seen their side tripped up by hugely inferior teams, came in the shape of the first visitors of the new year to Perry Barr. Burnley sat at the foot of the table and in eight away matches in '96/7 they had notched up just one point. The result was a foregone conclusion and, sure enough, Burnley hammered the Villa.

On New Year's Day, Liverpool caused a sensation by winning 4-1 at Bolton thus smashing the host side's unbeaten home record. That, though, was nothing compared to the disbelief which greeted news that Aston Villa had gone down 3-0 at home to Burnley on 2nd January.

The shockwaves created by the result were summed up by the *Birmingham Daily Post* which commented that the 14,000 crowd had: *"...gone to Perry Barr to see the first club in the League play the bottom club, and what sane individual could anticipate the victory of the latter. Anyone who had ventured that opinion prior to the contest would have been looked upon as a fool, afterwards a prophet."*

Burnley, it is true, played well above themselves and Tatham in goal was wonderful. The Villa forwards, meanwhile, were described as *"bungling"* in front of goal. The usual great understanding between the front men was not in evidence and passes regularly went astray while their shooting was terrible. Evans had come in at left-back as Crabtree was injured, and seven minutes into his return Albert saw Black score the opener from what looked suspiciously like an offside position.

Devey was unwell but played anyway. Quite simply, he shouldn't have done. A reserve could have done no worse and, with Devey below par in more ways than one, service to Athersmith was virtually nil. Even so, in the middle third of the game, it looked like Villa could win easily if they would just break out of the lethargy which had consumed the players.

It didn't happen and in the final half hour Villa were, according to press reports: *"...a disorganised and beaten combination."* Burnley recognised this and added two more goals before the end. First a mistake by Evans gifted the ball to Toman who beat Whitehouse. Bowes got the third before the referee put the home fans (and players) out of their misery. Only Spencer, Evans (despite his costly error) and Whitehouse came out of the game with any credit.

As if to mock Villa fans who had grown accustomed to being on the wrong end of 'shock' results, the next opponents, Sunderland, had been leapfrogged by Burnley thanks to the latter's win at Wellington Road. So it was to the bottom club

(again) that Villa travelled on 9th January. The game was said to be arousing great interest in the North East and the home club, in expectation of a record crowd, erected a temporary stand at their Newcastle Road enclosure. The kick-off was scheduled for 2.15 but would be delayed if necessary to give time for supporters to get into the ground.

There was no need. Having hugely over-estimated the attendance, just 8,000 turned up leaving match receipts at a lower than expected £230. Devey was absent for the first (and, as it turned out, last) time in '96/7. Crabtree returned to the side, this time in the inside-right position, while Albert Evans passed a late fitness test to line-up alongside Spencer at the back. In the half-back line, Reynolds was out with a leg strain handing Frank Burton his sixth start of the season. Chatt retained his spot at right-half leaving only Jas Cowan in place from the regular middle line.

These changes completely destroyed the balance of the team. Everything that could go wrong did go wrong. Whitehouse was abysmal until the final quarter of an hour when he was outstanding. Evans was weak (and not truly match fit) which meant Spencer, whilst performing brilliantly, was over-worked. Burton played badly and Chatt was fine defending but did little to help his forwards of whom only Athersmith and Crabtree came away from the game with any credit. The former crucified Gow at left-back but there was no one in the middle to receive his crosses. Yet despite all these faults, Villa had the greater share of possession, but an own goal from Ferguson and a good strike by Campbell were cancelled out by four goals from Sunderland who recorded only their second home win in ten games.

The less said about that 4-2 drubbing the better. The Villa were still on top of the League with a superior goal average to second placed Liverpool who had played four more games than the leaders.

Two days after the Sunderland debacle, Villa sent a weak eleven to Small Heath's Coventry Road ground to play a benefit for the home side's player, Walton, before 1,500 spectators. Reports described the mud as: *"ankle deep"* and the game as: *"little better than a farce."* Steve Smith scored Villa's goal in a 2-1 defeat.

The following Saturday Sunderland came to Birmingham to contest the return fixture with Aston Villa. The signs looked slightly better for a Villa win as their visitors had forced themselves off the bottom thanks to their efforts of a week earlier. The Villa team was:

Wilkes, Spencer, Crabtree, Reynolds, Jas Cowan, Chatt, Athersmith, Devey, Campbell,

Wheldon, Smith.

In a well contested first half, Wheldon struck the crossbar as Villa enjoyed the majority of possession, but the Sunderland backs kept the home team at bay with some fine defending. The interval came with the match goal-less. Within a minute of the re-start, however, Villa were in front. Wheldon charged 'keeper Doig and completed the job by chesting the ball home. The Villa inside-left thus took his goal tally for the season into double figures.

With 20 minutes to go, Sunderland levelled from a free-kick but Villa soon regained the lead. This time, the home side capitalised on a set piece which resulted in Devey rushing the ball home and the match ended with a 2-1 win for Villa, their first of 1897. It was by no means a classic encounter but came as a welcome relief to Aston Villa as an alarming slump had been halted before it had chance to gain momentum.

The team put in a below par performance although there were a few pluses to take from the ninety minutes. Wilkes showed up well in goal. The half-backs were fine apart from some very poor shooting, with Reynolds being the worst offender. Athersmith was on top form despite the close attentions of Gow who, it must be said, was glad that he wouldn't have to face Villa's lightning fast winger again this season.

* * *

The next first-class competitive match the Villa were due to take part in would again pit the 'Pets' against opposition from the North East. FA Cup 1st round day was fast approaching and second division Newcastle United were to be the visitors to Wellington Road. The Villa's programme leading up to the game involved a 23rd January friendly at Tottenham Hotspur (then a Southern League side) and yet another visit to Stoney Lane two days later where West Brom stood between Villa and the 3rd round of the Birmingham Senior Cup. Meanwhile, Newcastle United were undergoing special preparation for the tie.

Heavy snow greeted the Villa team as they paraded themselves in the capital city for the third time this season, even so 3,000 came to watch the game. Apart from their brilliant play, Villa attracted large attendances in London because they were one of the few clubs who used tours of the city to play football rather than, as was often the case with others, an excuse to hit the bright lights.

The Spurs match was no exception and the fans left in good heart having seen Villa turn on the style in a display of exhibition football. An additional reason for the Londoners to smile was that their team, despite twice going behind to Charlie Athersmith strikes, fought back well to earn a two-all draw.

Snow was, again, the major feature of the match at West Brom. There was 3" of it on the pitch. A weakened Villa side relinquished their hold on the Birmingham Senior Cup as they fell to a 2-1 defeat. Had Devey and Griffiths been more accurate, however, that result may have been different. Instead, three visits to Stoney Lane by the Champions had yielded nothing better than three losses.

Unusually, Aston Villa didn't seem to be too bothered about the local trophies in '96/7. This may have been because they genuinely believed they had a chance of the Double and decided that, if they were going to equal Preston North End's feat of 1889, they would have to rest key players in the minor competitions. If that was the plan, the first test of it came on Saturday 30th January as the world's most famous knockout tournament properly got under way.

Having paid the collective sum of £196, a small crowd of 6,000 braved heavy rain to witness the start of Villa's historic English Cup run. The game was in doubt because sheets of water covered the pitch. The turnstiles were not opened until late because the referee wanted to be sure the game could be completed before he would okay the playing surface. Eventually the punters were allowed in and the players got changed in the Blacksmith's Yard across Wellington Road from the ground. The game was on. The team which began Villa's 1897 Cup run was:

Wilkes, Spencer, Evans, Chatt, Jas Cowan, Crabtree, Athersmith, Devey, Campbell, Wheldon, Smith.

The game, despite the conditions, saw Villa at their best. After a quarter of an hour, Devey played the ball beyond the Newcastle left-back White who simply couldn't keep up with the on-rushing Athersmith. Charlie found the target with a beautifully placed shot. Then it was Wheldon's turn to score. He showed great control in taking a strong pass from Smith and shot low into the far corner of the net.

Two minutes later, Wheldon again unleashed a shot which rebounded off a Newcastle United defender. Smith - who possessed excellent reflexes - was first to the rebound and took full advantage to put his side three up. The report in the *Birmingham Daily Post* said: *"It was a case now of the Villa first and Newcastle nowhere."*

A minute before the interval, Wheldon swung in a corner kick. White tried to clear but the ball skidded off his boot and into the net giving Villa a 4-0 half-time lead. That could have been more but for some desperate defending by the visiting backs.

In the second half, United came into the game more and tested Wilkes on at least half a dozen occasions. But the Villa still held the upper hand and how the visitors goal remained unbreached for so long is anyone's guess. Having ridden their luck throughout the second half, however, Newcastle finally conceded a fifth two minutes from time when Wheldon got his second goal of the game following a fast break from Athersmith.

Even on a terrible pitch, the Villa forwards passed perfectly. All the players came off covered in mud although Devey was in a worse state than anyone else. He unintentionally got the crowd laughing when, having attempted a sliding tackle, he kept going, skidding for three yards on his backside. His comic capers aside, the Villa skipper fed Athersmith well throughout and the winger made some remarkable runs deep into enemy territory.

Campbell dropped deep and used the wings well while Wheldon's dribbling confused the life out of the unfortunate United backs. He also made numerous openings for Steve Smith who, by his standards, had an indifferent game despite his well taken goal.

The halves did their job perfectly, tackling uncompromisingly, feeding their forwards and shooting with accuracy. Crabtree, especially, forced numerous saves from the Newcastle 'keeper. At the back, Evans had an excellent, if quiet, game, Wilkes was faultless and Spencer simply majestic. The latter read the game brilliantly and was always in the right place at the right time.

About Newcastle, it has to be said that they weren't the power they would become. By the time the FA Cup draw next threw the two teams together for the 1905 final, United had become the richest (or at least most profitable) club in the country. In 1897, the Geordies were still growing and simply couldn't live with the big boys. A miserable 1st round was completed for them when they got the bill for competing in the tie. It had cost £50 just to send the players to a training camp. What with travelling expenses as well, they lost money on the tie even after they had received their share of the gate. It would have been infinitely preferable to have suffered such a big defeat at home!

* * *

January was definitely an indifferent month for Aston Villa, regardless of how well they ended it. As well as finding themselves in the hat for the second round of the Cup, they had survived a cou-

ple of hiccups to retain top spot in the League with two-thirds of the campaign behind them:

	pld	home					away					g.av	pts
		w	d	l	f	a	w	d	l	f	a		
1 Aston Villa	20	6	2	2	19	13	6	2	2	24	16	1.48	28
2 Liverpool	24	6	4	1	19	6	5	2	6	20	22	1.39	28
3 Derby	22	10	1	2	43	19	2	2	5	11	18	1.46	27
4 Everton	20	6	1	3	27	15	5	2	3	15	14	1.45	25
5 Sheff U	20	5	4	3	21	11	3	4	1	11	8	1.68	24
6 Preston	19	7	2	1	29	15	1	5	3	11	11	1.53	23
7 Bolton	19	5	2	1	15	7	4	2	5	14	15	1.32	22
8 Sheff W	21	6	2	2	22	10	1	5	5	14	15	1.32	22
9 W Brom	23	6	2	5	14	12	3	3	4	11	24	0.69	21
10 N Forest	22	7	2	2	24	10	0	3	8	9	28	0.87	19
11 Blackburn	22	6	1	4	19	17	2	2	7	5	30	0.51	19
12 Wolves	21	4	2	5	18	12	2	2	6	12	17	1.03	16
13 Bury	18	3	4	1	14	10	1	4	5	9	21	0.74	16
14 Stoke	21	3	3	3	15	13	3	0	9	16	34	0.65	15
15 Burnley	19	3	5	2	15	13	1	1	7	12	25	0.71	14
16 Sunderland	23	2	4	4	12	15	2	2	9	11	25	0.58	14

At the top of the table, Liverpool were clinging on to second place having completed more of their programme than any other team. Everton were creeping up menacingly while Derby, Sheffield United and Preston North End were staying in touch. Bolton had hit a rotten patch of form which had seen them slip from first to seventh after picking up just one point from five games. But atop them all were the Villa team who had rediscovered the winning formula.

In the Cup, holders Sheffield Wednesday fell at the first hurdle after narrowly losing to Forest while in-form Liverpool just scraped through by the odd goal in seven against Burton Swifts. Bolton's woes continued when they were held goalless by second division Grimsby. A similar lack of goals was the story of Bury's visit to non-league Stockton. Meanwhile, Villa's opponents in the next round would be Notts County who defeated Small Heath in an all-Division Two clash.

Difficulties in dealing with the bottom clubs aside, Villa's season was looking good and they had come through the tough festive period to find themselves in a position which was the envy of the rest of football. If the campaign so far had been more than satisfactory, what was to come was truly awesome.

Chapter Six

A League To Win And A Man To Win It
William McGregor and Joseph Grierson

In 1847, a lady of Braco, a village in Perthshire, gave birth to a boy who would one day take an essentially British pastime and turn it into the world's number one sport. That boy was William McGregor. His first taste of the game that would consume his every waking moment came at the tender age of seven, when he saw twenty-two men chasing round a meadow and doing beastly things to a poor, innocent leather sphere. He was hooked.

Skipping through the early years, we next catch up with McGregor as the 23 year old Scot was surveying his new home. He had moved to the great, and rapidly expanding, city of Birmingham. A draper by profession, this canny businessman soon built a thriving company with premises in Newtown's notorious Summer Lane. Yet, despite having to make a living, he somehow found time to help the Villa, and the sport they excelled at, become revered the planet over.

It was in the very early days of the Club that McGregor first began to shape the fortunes of Aston Villa. Certainly, it was no later than 1876 (two years after that famous 'gaslight' meeting in Heathfield Road) for he, along with George Kynoch MP, were guarantors for the lease on the Wellington Road enclosure. This was the first major act of a man who, despite scaling the heights as football's most famous administrator, never lost sight of the fact that he was essentially a football fan - more particularly, Aston Villa's number one fan.

In its early days, the Club was run in a similar way to modern nonleague outfits. Today, so many semi-professional clubs have a chairman who doubles up as groundsman, maintenance man, bar steward, kit washer and coach driver. During his association with the Villa club, this is precisely what William McGregor did. He had no specific role, rather he did whatever was needed. He was always on-hand to offer assistance at any time as this quote from the man himself confirms: *"I can recall more than one match* (at Wellington Road) *where there were only two spectators; myself and George Ramsay's brother."*

Wherever the Villa were, with them was McGregor. He accompanied the team on their leg-endary tours around the British Isles, during which he had the unenviable task of trying to keep order. His recollections of those excursions to the far flung corners of the kingdom were happy ones:

"In the old days the social side of the Club was one of its most pronounced characteristics. The tours they used to take in Scotland were productive of more fun than any journeys I have ever read of. There was a wonderfully strong bond of fellowship in those days among footballers, and I have never come across a happier band of brothers than Aston Villa were."

McGregor was in charge when the team undertook perhaps their most famed tour North of the Border, a trip which resulted in an undesirable entry in the Aston Villa record book. It was the last two weeks of February 1889 that Aston Villa took on the creme of Scottish football. They also took on the ale and spirits of that fair land as matches became an unwelcome diversion from the real work - drinking. By the time an exhausted McGregor dragged his charges back to Birmingham, the fine athletes that had left the fine city had become a bedraggled bunch. Hardly ideal preparation for the FA Cup 3rd round tie in which Villa were due to do battle with a free-scoring Blackburn Rovers side. The 8-1 scoreline from that match still stands as Villa's heaviest defeat and everyone who witnessed the game put the reversal down to the complete lack of fitness and awareness of the visiting Villans.

So trips to his homeland were not always relaxing holidays - for McGregor at least! He was especially scathing about the lack of discipline amongst his fellow countrymen, particularly in the early days of professional football. He commented that the Scottish players who came down to England had to be watched all the time because given half a chance they would be out on the town. It should be noted, however, that by the 1896/7 season, professional footballers - particularly those employed by Aston Villa - evinced a professional attitude and most did not need to be nannied.

Yet the Double year couldn't have happened but for the amazing vision of William McGregor, as the 'Double' would not have existed. In the 1880's a number of local cup competitions and, of course, the English Cup provided competitive football for clubs but most games took the form of hastily arranged friendlies. Crowds at some of these matches were pitifully low, partly because there was nothing but pride at stake but also because it was a matter of luck as to whether teams would field their strongest elevens or, indeed, even turn up. Many was the time when a team scheduled to play at Perry Barr on a Saturday would get word to the club late on the preceding Friday that they were unable to fulfil the fixture. Sometimes replacement opposition would be found, at other times supporters would turn up at Wellington Road to be greeted by 'Game Off' signs. In such circumstances, it was hardly surprising that fans stayed away.

These factors and more were brought home to William McGregor whilst he was in a coffee-shop situated next door to his Summer Lane premises. The owner of the cafe was Villa supporter Joe Tillotson who complained bitterly about the number of games which were cancelled and also claimed that fans were sick of one-sided friendly matches. McGregor realised that the complaints of the fans had to be dealt with if the sport was to maintain the momentum of its growing popularity. The answer he came up with was The Football League.

William McGregor first presented his 'League' idea to two Villa Committee members in 1886. In the lounge of the Old Crown & Cushion, Joshua Margoschis (Club chairman in the Double year) and Charles Fergus Johnstone (original director and former Villa left-back) enthusiastically gave the thumbs up to the grand plan. From there, and with the backing of his Football Club, McGregor worked tirelessly to group the top clubs together in a regular competition.

He travelled the country to put his proposal to the game's giants, not all of whom shared his vision. Sheffield Wednesday feared that the FA would come down hard on any clubs which joined such a scheme and which might threaten the absolute power held by football's governing body. Nottingham Forest, meanwhile, saw the League as a threat to their amateur status which they were desperate to cling to.

But McGregor's argument won many supporters. His logic was astoundingly simple: Professionalism had become a reality and with it had come wage bills. The only way for a top club to meet its high costs was via regular gates which *"had become imperative."* Getting the leading sides to play each other in a regulated competition was the only way to realise this.

On 2nd March 1888, William McGregor sent out the following circular:

"Every year it is becoming more and more difficult for football clubs of any standing to meet their friendly engagements, and even arrange friendly matches. The consequence is that at the last moment, through cup-tie interferences, clubs are compelled to take on teams who will not attract the public. I beg to tender the following suggestion as a means of getting over the difficulty. That ten or twelve of the most prominent clubs in England combine to arrange home-and-away fixtures each season, the said fixtures to be arranged at a friendly conference about the same time as the International Conference. This combination might be known as the Association Football Union, and could be managed by a representative from each club. Of course, this is in no way to interfere with the National Association; even the suggested matches might be played under cup-tie rules. However, this is a detail. My object in writing you at present is merely to draw your attention to the subject, and to suggest a friendly conference to discuss the matter more fully. I would take it as a favour if you would kindly think the matter over, and make whatever suggestion you may deem necessary. I am only writing to the following: Blackburn Rovers, Bolton Wanderers, Preston North End, West Bromwich Albion and Aston Villa, and should like to hear what other clubs you would suggest.

I am, yours very truly,
William McGregor.

P.S. - How would Friday, March 23, 1888, suit for the friendly conference at Anderton's Hotel, London?

All five clubs favourably replied and the friendly conference took place with the 'originals' joined by representatives from Accrington, Burnley, Wolves, Stoke City and Notts County. The meeting unanimously agreed to the formation of the Football League. A second gathering took place at Manchester's Royal Hotel on 17th April 1888 at which the group of ten clubs was expanded to include Derby County and Everton. The latter accepted the invitation to join when it was decided that gate money from League matches should be pooled. At the time, Everton were not as powerful as the other eleven clubs but it didn't take them long to catch up and overtake many.

Other clubs wished to join but it was decided that only 22 'free' weekends could be guaranteed so only a dozen teams began a competition which has survived and prospered to the present day. Further, McGregor's visionary idea has been adopted by all sports and travelled to the four corners of the globe. It was such a simple scheme, yet it transformed the game and took it to unprecedented heights of popularity and prosperity.

Not everyone was favourably disposed to

McGregor's grand design with some even object-ing to the word 'league'. But the Father of the League (as McGregor came to be known the world over) once admitted he found such people: "...brainless asses - although that being too strong a term, 'foolish people' would suffice." He also had this to say about those who held deeper suspi-cions about the League and its effect on the game:

"People who rail at the League forget the state football was in at the time that the League was founded. It is a very easy matter to rail at the League, but if some of these wiseacres had been responsible for football government at the time I introduced the system, they would have known that something of the kind was essential."

Another great administrator of the day, Bolton's J.J. Bentley who held senior positions at the League and FA, explained further: *" . . . open pro-fessionalism looked like spelling financial ruin to the clubs which embraced it, and the turning point came when Mr. W. McGregor of Birmingham sug-gested the League system... and the early devel-opment of it saved professional football, and very soon popularised it."*

William McGregor

Having saved the game from at best stagnation and at worst collapse, William McGregor continued to work tirelessly for the sport he loved. At the turn of the Century he simultaneously held the following posts: Member of the Birmingham FA and its rep-resentative on the National FA Council, member of the FA Finance Committee, Vice-President of the Staffordshire FA and the Football League, President of both the Birmingham Youths and Old Boys' Association and the Birmingham Junior Charity Association. He also at the time sat on the Appeals Committee of the Staffordshire FA and the Birmingham and District League.

At Aston Villa, he was a vice-president although he had served the Club in nearly every administrative capacity at one time or another, including a spell as Committee Chairman when Villa first won the English Cup in 1887. His incredi-ble vision was also in evidence on a smaller scale at his favourite club. We have already noted that he organised the transportation of Villa fans to away matches, but he also suggested the Club be made a limited liability company, years before it actually happened. It didn't go down well as this comment from McGregor shows:

"...people howled when I proposed this; but then people will howl at anything which is novel."

McGregor didn't expect everyone to be a visionary like himself but he had no time for those who, through fear or ignorance, would not embrace innovation. Normally a very easy-going man, despite his austere appearance, he was a strong believer in the power of logic and refused to suffer in silence those who practised dogmatism and intransigence.

Despite never claiming to possess the football brain of George Ramsay, McGregor also had ideas which helped to get the most out of the play-ers at the Club. In the modern era which has tend-ed to forget the great men of the past, Sir Matt Busby is often credited with developing the 'youth' system in professional football. The truth is some-what different for, in a rousing speech at Aston Villa's Annual General Meeting of 1897, McGregor said that he hoped there would be more emphasis on junior teams, a comment that led to the Villa - with the help of William McGregor - implementing the first proper scouting and youth policy, which became the forerunner of today's schools of excel-lence.

The football of the 1990's owes so much to McGregor's vision, but it is unlikely that he would have had much time for the people who run the modern game. Two quotes give substance to such an assumption, the first being McGregor's thoughts on the role and power of the League which, when read, should be compared to the poli-tics of today's Premiership:

"A league should never aspire to be a govern-ing body. There was a time when I was disposed to think... that the League should govern profes-sional football; but, after all, I have come to see that it is best for the whole government of football to be in the hands of the Football Association. . . . The League have their own work to do; they have to look after their own interests, but they should not seek to govern. A body whose aims are neces-sarily selfish, as those of the League are, ought not to desire to be a governing body. When the League meet, they are actuated by the interests of

the League clubs. The general good of football is not then their chief concern."

The second statement from William McGregor, which many a modern football club director would rather wasn't aired, highlights perfectly the difference between the men who guided our clubs through the early days of professional football and those who today are, in so many cases, responsible for divorcing those same institutions from the local communities and the fans who are the essence of the clubs. In 1905 he wrote:

"...directors cannot be remunerated for their services. The FA very rightly insists that the men who run football clubs shall do so as a matter of sentiment. (This) is wise because it brings into the work the right class of men - that is to say, men who love football for its own sake... I can tell you candidly that the position of football director of a League club carries with it an amount of work which, if any man looked at it through business spectacles, would call for heavy remuneration. But it would be a bad day for football if you divorced the sportsman and substituted for him the guineapig, or the man who does not mind doing any work that he is well remunerated for."

The current football world would not please the Father of the League. Then again, were he alive today, it is likely the game would be much different as he would not have allowed the clubs - or at least his club - to move so far away from their main sponsors: the supporters. Sadly, we will never know what might be with a modern McGregor because, quite simply, his kind does not exist anymore.

At the beginning of December 1911, football's greatest visionary died at Miss Storer's Nursing Home. In tribute to the departed 64 year old Father of the League, his friend Harry Doe wrote on the 11th of that same month: "All of us are sorry he has gone and everyone of his old cronies will miss him sorely because of his at once genial company and unfailing optimism... His memory will remain as fresh and green as the grass that grows over him."

* * *

The League was good for Aston Villa. Apart from being the key to regular fixtures and resultant regular income, it also gave the Club a new competition to dominate. But to win the League, particularly in the 1890's when it was a much more open affair than it is today, a special kind of man was needed to hone a club's talent. To win it again and again required that man to be a genius.

It was rare that a club would poach a coach from a rival outfit - again unlike today. But that is precisely what Aston Villa did in 1893. John Devey had been groomed to take care of matters on the pitch, and George Ramsay scouted for the players who would best fit the Villa style: a style that had been developed from his own playing days, through the reign of the incomparable Archie Hunter, before being perfected in the glory decade. There was one missing link and Middlesbrough Ironopolis had possession of it. So Ramsay went to the North-East and returned with a trainer: the one and only Joe Grierson.

One could be forgiven for asking: "Joe who?" because he has been overlooked by football historians, Villa fans and, worst of all, the Villa Club, ever since the First World War brought to an end his incredible association with Aston Villa. It is difficult to find out much about a man who was very much in the background in his heyday and has continued to remain well away from the public eye despite his remarkable achievements. What little is known about him and his coaching methods is worthy of recording. There may even be a few modern-day managers who would like to know his secret.

As has been mentioned, Villa had a unique style of play. Others tried to copy it but failed to perform in the polished manner of the Kings of English Football. This meant that players who were brought into the Club, be they at youth or senior level, had to be re-trained in the Villa method. In the first few years of the 1890's, there was no one who could do this job adequately. Hence, the team of that time did not trouble trophy engravers.

In general, the job of team trainer was, for many years, simply one of getting the players fit by organising their running, exercises and weight training. Tactics and skills were left to the players themselves and if anyone directed the 'football' coaching sessions it would be a Committee member or the captain.

Grierson certainly got his charges into the peak of condition. In a later chapter, the activities he arranged when the players went to training camps to prepare for big games are detailed. The run of the mill sessions involved plenty of running, either in the form of races or combined with basic ball control. He also supervised the use of weights rather than, as was the norm, leave the men to lift whatever and whenever they felt like lifting. The first key to Joe's - and the Villa's - success was organisation. The training sessions looked the same as those undertaken by every other club, but Aston Villa's were planned and well supervised. In short, everything the players did was done for a reason.

The same organisational skills were utilised

when it came to the task of turning a mere foot-baller into a 'Villa' player. Albert Evans inadvertent-ly summed up the difference between the two when he said that he and his team-mates would adapt themselves to the methods employed by the opposition at any given time. John Devey would, according to Evans, quickly work out what the other side were trying to do and develop a style to counter the opponents' plan. This required an enormous amount of versatility in the play of each individual and, more than that, tremendous under-standing of each other's roles in various tactical formations.

Joe Grierson

Here again, it was Joe Grierson who made sure that the players were both highly competent at their own jobs and possessed an awareness of each constituent part of the whole team. He did this by training the different departments of the team in isolation one day, and then bringing them all together the next. This switching of schedules not only rendered the sessions enjoyable but also meant that every member of the squad became expert in his own job and was at least theoretically knowledgeable about all the positions.

He was one of the first coaches to impose spe-cialist training on goalkeepers. Wilkes, Whitehouse and George would spend a few hours a week sav-ing shots, working out angles and completing spe-cially designed stretching exercises. All three pos-sessed an incredible agility which was testament to the work put in on the training ground.

Similarly, the backs and halves would have the importance of timing tackles drummed into them. And the forwards were taught the value of support-ing the man with the ball, making dummy runs, tak-ing defenders away from the play and moving into space after releasing the ball. All this sounds very basic but for a couple of years until the rest of foot-

ball woke up to what was going on at Perry Barr, the Villa were the only team who did these things. Middlesbrough Ironopolis, having enjoyed Grierson's services, no doubt tried similar methods but they did not possess the players to make the system work so well, hence they were consistently foiled in their attempts to gain entry into the sec-ond division.

Once each player completely understood his position, he was ready to become acquainted with the system. In addition to the sectionalised train-ing, the whole squad would get together and learn what they were expected to do when the side was attacking and when defending. An example of a typical moment during a typical game best high-lights the benefit of the hours spent working with Grierson:

Jas Cowan times a tackle to perfection and is left with the ball at his feet. Just behind and to the side would be his two wing-halfs who had been covering Jas as he made his challenge. They would push out towards the wings should a side-ways pass be Cowan's best option. The two full-backs would push up in order to catch forwards offside should the opposition win the ball back and try a quick break. The wingers start to move down the flanks where they would either find room for themselves or stretch the enemy defence leaving space for the inside-forwards to exploit. Directly in front of Jas, John Campbell would drop deep to receive the ball.

The options for the centre-half were numerous. If he played it to Campbell, the forward could either turn and go towards goal himself, or he could knock the ball back to an inside-forward or wing-half: the team's dribblers. Another option would be to spread play out to the wingers. But what if Jas still has the ball and the opposition has done its job and all the Villa players are being tightly marked? Simple. Jas knows - because he has done it thou-sands of times on the training ground - that he has to play the ball behind the opponents left-back. Meanwhile, Charlie Athersmith has seen that Jas has no one free to play the ball to and has got up a head of steam down the right flank. The result of Jas' and Charlie's instinctive play: Athersmith and ball meet and the poor full-back is left desperately puffing as Villa's winger hares past him.

Whatever situation arose in a match, every Villa player knew what he had to do and what his comrades would be doing. The only time the sys-tem failed was when a number of the team were off their game, a rare occurrence. Quite simply - and apart from Ramsay's astute purchases - the secret ingredient behind Villa's success, the rea-son they could play a beautiful game of ground passing and sweeping balls to the wide men, and why other clubs tried and failed to copy the Lions' style, was the training regime devised by Joe Grierson.

The proof of Joe's greatness is his record of achievement. To fully appreciate his successes, it is worth looking at the following record and asking what one's attitude would be to a manager who could boast such triumphs today. Grierson spent twenty-two seasons with the Villa during which time the League was conquered six times, the FA Cup won four times, the Double completed once and nearly repeated when the FA Cup was won in 1913 and Villa finished second in the League. The Club were also runners-up on four other occasions. And the Cup wins in 1895 and 1905 saw Aston Villa finish their Division One seasons in third and fourth places respectively.

The only managers who have achieved a comparable level of sustained success are Herbert Chapman, Sir Matt Busby, Bill Shankly and Bob Paisley. That is the company which Joe Grierson keeps. And to think people - even Villa people - ask *"Joe who?"*

Victorian Villa was a happy close-knit community, yet Grierson seemed a bit of an outsider. He threw his heart and soul into his job and, where George Ramsay, William McGregor, James Lees, even Fred Rinder and the rest of the Committee would join the players for a drink and let their hair down, Joe it appears never got too close to anyone at the Club. His flat-cap became a trademark and, in all likelihood, the players he helped to achieve greatness knew as much about the man's headgear as they did about the man himself.

Joe Grierson set a standard which every Aston Villa manager has had to live up to. Some may think that unfair but, when success has been the norm, one tends to start expecting greatness and rejecting anything less. The fact that none of his successors has come close to emulating Mr. Grierson's achievements may go some way to explaining why there have been so many of them!

Chapter Seven

We Never Lose

Going into February Bury and Burnley, Aston Villa's next two opponents, were sitting in thirteenth and fifteenth places respectively. As an added inducement, the Villa Committee promised the players a bonus of £5 each if they came back from these away games with maximum points. The results of these matches were by no means a foregone conclusion as exemplified by Villa's record against weaker sides. Bury issued a further warning to any complacent Villa men by beginning the month with a 12-1 slaughter of non-league Stockton in their Cup 1st round replay.

Saturday 6th February saw Villa take on the 'Team of Surprises', as Bury had become known. The Gigg Lane team had reason to fancy their chances having drawn at Perry Barr three months earlier. Many in the 10,000 crowd were hoping that Bury could repeat their greatest triumph when they beat the Champions 5-3 in the corresponding fixture the season before. They would go home disappointed.

The same Villa line-up that comprehensively defeated Newcastle in the Cup took to the soft, slippery Gigg Lane pitch and, having won the toss, chose to play with what little wind there was. Bury started well enough but soon Villa upped the pace and took the game to their hosts. As the first half wore on the Bury goal began to be bombarded, with Crabtree, Athersmith and Wheldon all going close.

The breakthrough came in the 34th minute. Devey had been the latest Villa man to trouble Montgommery, the Bury 'keeper, and the danger was never really cleared. A clever passing move involving all the forwards ended with the ball being laid back to John Campbell some 25 yards out and his first time shot rocketed into the top corner. Two minutes later and the centre-forward scored again, this time from closer range. This completed the scoring for the match as Villa gave a demonstration of 'keep-ball' that would grace any European Cup game.

The ease of the victory - for nearly an hour Bury only had proper control of the ball when they kicked-off - put the Villa players and the travelling faithful in good heart for the trip to Burnley two days later. This was Villa's chance to avenge the

embarrassing defeat suffered at Perry Barr the month before.

The crowd only just reached 5,000 and nearly a quarter of them were Villa fans. Burnley were having an abysmal season which, though they didn't know it at the time, was going to get a whole lot worse. 1895/6 had been a decidedly average campaign for the home side but they would have greatly appreciated a return to mediocrity this time round. They had already suffered first round exit in the Cup and, come April, they were relegated after the Test Matches having finished bottom of Division One.

Again no team changes for the Villa who played downhill in the first half on a very heavy pitch. Fortunately, this time the game was completed although the intermittent rain must have made the small crowd think that, once again, Burnley versus Aston Villa would be abandoned.

Villa were quickest out of the blocks and Tatham was forced to make two excellent saves in the opening couple of minutes. One of these followed a blistering run from Athersmith that saw him cover 60 yards before the home defence had a chance to get close enough to even attempt a tackle. That was a prelude to John Campbell's 4th minute close-range header which put Villa in front.

Burnley came back at Villa immediately and Toman sliced a shot from near the corner flag which took Wilkes by surprise, but the Villa custodian made a save albeit with some difficulty. It was Villa's turn to attack and they showed the home side how to take chances when, again, Campbell found the net. It was a flowing move down the right between Devey and Athersmith which set up the Scottish centre-forward who placed his shot well from 10 yards out.

The play switched from end to end. In one half of the pitch, McLintock and Robertson caused the Villa backs a fair amount of trouble while, at the other end, Athersmith was a one man wrecking machine, tearing through the Burnley defences and bringing the best out of Tatham with some excellent shots. Villa gradually got on top and, five minutes from the break, Campbell completed his hat-trick after Athersmith (who else?) had left three defenders on their backsides as he once again single-handedly skinned the home side. On the stroke of half-time, Robertson handed Burnley a lifeline when he beat Wilkes following a goal-mouth scramble.

From the re-start, Burnley cut through the Villa and a left-wing Toman cross went straight into the net. Wilkes hadn't learned his lesson from Toman's earlier effort from an acute angle and the 'keeper found himself hopelessly out of position as the home team reduced the deficit to one.

Villa, though, looked the stronger outfit and, after a period of sustained pressure by the visitors, Steve Smith curled a delightful ball into the path of Devey whose first time shot left Tatham with no chance. Meanwhile, at the other end, Evans was limping badly following a strong challenge by Robertson, but the backs and halves were coping well with Burnley's rushes. The Villa sat back a little but kept hitting their opponents on the break and were it not for a magnificent display by Tatham, a huge score would have been run-up by the Pets' marauding forwards.

Yet it was Burnley who would get the only other goal of the match. The last ten minutes saw the home side pen Villa back in an attempt to salvage something from the game. Black managed to reduce the arrears but the Villa contained their opponents well and ended with a 4-3 win. Thus the players got their £5 bonuses for securing two wins in two matches. The game, which was a hugely enjoyable spectacle, was not quite as close as the scoreline suggested. The Villa forwards were far too clever for Burnley who had Tatham to thank for saving them from humiliation. He had a faultless game yet still had four put past him; a sign of how well the Villa front-line performed. At the back, the injury to Evans did not help Villa's cause and nor did Wilkes' misreading of his angles. Still, even though their 'goal average' column wasn't as high as it might have been, two points was all Villa needed and they got them in style.

* * *

It was time to return to FA Cup action on 13th February as Notts County came to Perry Barr. A Villa win was expected and after the way the team had dealt with second division opposition in the 1st round, a sack-full of goals was also being predicted by many in the season-low 4,000 crowd.

It didn't quite work out like that. The first half was a desperate struggle with both teams having their share of chances but neither looking dominant. County, playing downhill with the wind, were first into their stride and regularly troubled the Villa backs. Only five minutes had elapsed when Campbell was penalised for a late challenge with the resultant free-kick giving County the lead.

The Villa team was often prone to take supposedly lesser opposition lightly and the signs were that they had done so with Notts County. Yet, as with all great sides, Aston Villa were never so dangerous as when they fell behind and the visitors' goal stung the home side into life. The forwards took control of the game with Athersmith playing his customary 'blinder'. It was he and Devey who, with lovely passing and movement, carried the ball deep into Notts territory on the quarter hour. Charlie whipped in a cross which Wheldon beautifully controlled before placing it past Toone to level matters.

Ten minutes later Bramley, the County right-half, collided with James Crabtree leaving the former nursing a fractured right shin. The cracking of the bone could be heard in the press box some 20 yards away from the incident and the injury was so horrific that several spectators fainted. Up until the collision, the game looked like being a corker but play degenerated from that point onwards. All the players seemed to be affected by what had happened to Bramley, none more so than Crabtree who understandably didn't seem to have the desire to continue. His tackling certainly carried less bite from then on.

At the start of the second half, even with the wind behind them, Villa found it hard to get to grips with the game and County gained the ascendancy. Wilkes was kept busy at one end while, at the other, the home forwards were shooting badly. Allan and Langham, Notts' right-wing pair, were causing no end of problems for the Villa backs. In one glorious run, Langham broke out of defence and raced three-quarters of the length of the field, beating Crabtree and Evans on the way. He hit a cracking shot which Wilkes matched for brilliance by tipping the goal-bound effort away at full stretch.

Midway through the half Villa started to get on top and, for a five minute period, were camped in the visitors' goal-mouth. But it wasn't until the 85th minute that Villa took a controversial lead. Athersmith swung in a corner which looked like going straight in. Campbell raced between two defenders and just got a toe to it. Had the Scotsman's intervention come before the ball crossed the line? Referee John Lewis said yes. The Notts County players said no. The press said it was: *"...a very close decision."*

So Aston Villa scraped through to the third round. Wilkes played very well and Reynolds had a good match having come back at the expense of Bob Chatt. Other than that pair, only the wingers showed up favourably for the home side. Smith continued his good form which prompted the

International Board to select him for the forthcoming England match against Ireland. Sadly for the player, he picked up a knock in the Notts County game and was unable to play for his country.

But the match of 13th February would be remembered for the injury to Bramley; the first player in 14 years to break his leg at Perry Barr. During the match a collection was taken by the crowd for the unfortunate County man. The incident obviously had a detrimental effect on the game although the Committee put Villa's poor performance down to fatigue after the hard games at Bury and Burnley.

Elsewhere in the Cup second round, Wolves and West Brom bowed out to Blackburn and Liverpool respectively, leaving Villa to carry the flag for the West Midlands.

* * *

The quarter-final draw for the FA Cup sent Villa away from home, something which will come as no surprise to today's fans. But before they could travel to Preston North End's Deepdale enclosure for the 27th February tie, they had to concentrate on the League match scheduled for five days earlier when Perry Barr would welcome the visit of... Preston North End.

Following obvious signs of tiredness in recent games, the Committee were determined that the team should be in the best possible condition as their push for Double glory reached a critical stage. So, under the direction of James Lees and Joe Grierson, the players were sent off to a training camp to prepare for the struggles against the, then, only Club to have achieved the Double.

Club director James Lees had taken over from William McGregor the job of chaperoning the team on tours and to training camps. The choice of Lees probably resulted from the fearsome physical stature of the man. He was built like the proverbial brick outhouse and this alone should have persuaded the players that they were not to step out of line. Gone was the era of all-night parties on Club tours as such activities would have incurred the wrath of the man who looked like a caricature of a nightclub bouncer.

On Thursday 18th February 1897, Lees and Grierson led the squad to Droitwich where the players enjoyed a salt bath. They then moved on to Holt Fleet where they would undergo light training. On the Friday, they were given the day off to relax. Athersmith and Wheldon meanwhile travelled to Nottingham to join up with the England team for Saturday's contest with Ireland.

Saturday at Holt Fleet was spent doing some light running. To keep up interest and improve the team's skills, Joe Grierson set up some dribbling races - something at which George Ramsay won many awards during his playing days. Meanwhile, over at the famous Trent Bridge ground, 13,000 spectators represented a record crowd for the Irish international match which saw England run out 6-0 winners.

Wheldon, making his England debut, scored the first three goals, the culmination of his hat-trick being a brilliant swerve-shot from an incredibly acute angle. He also missed an easier chance presented by an Athersmith cross. Charlie himself set up three and scored the last of England's six goals. The ball was played forward but Derby's Steve Bloomer (who played inside right) knew he was in an offside position. Scott, the Irish 'keeper, started to come out but hesitated when he saw that Bloomer was making no attempt to get to the ball. This gave Athersmith enough time to nip in and guide his shot into the unguarded net.

The Villa pair returned to Holt Fleet having had a brilliant day out representing their country. Wheldon's joy at his debut hat-trick was, however, dampened slightly by the news that the selectors had not picked him for the Scotland match.

After another day of mainly fitness training, the team left for Birmingham on Monday 22nd for their 23rd League game of the season. The same eleven that accounted for Notts County started the game, but the larger squad was depleted as Bob Chatt had a nasty foot injury which eventually required the attention of Manchester's medical marvel, Mr. Whitehead. A crowd of nearly 20,000 packed Wellington Road hoping to get some clues as to the probable result of the Cup tie due to be contested between the two famous clubs on the upcoming Saturday.

In the first half, Villa outplayed North End. Athersmith, Crabtree and Smith were on top form and Jas Cowan would have been a candidate for man of the match but for the return of his 'Skyscraper'. Time and again he troubled the pigeons with his wayward shooting. For Preston, James Trainer was outstanding but, being the goalkeeper, he had to be.

Villa kicked-off playing uphill and, after Boycott and Boyd had given the home supporters scares in the first minute, they took the game to the visitors. Wheldon went on a mazey dribble before finding Smith. The winger crossed but Wheldon couldn't direct his header. Villa were nearly made to regret that lost opportunity when Preston launched a counter-attack through Boyd and Henderson. They set up Stephenson who shot over when he had a virtual open goal to aim at.

But in the 13th minute, the Villa pressure told when Smith crossed from the left and Devey was on hand to beat Trainer. Devey thus joined Campbell and Wheldon in reaching double figures for League goals. Further, his strike represented Villa's 50th score in the League for '96/7. More importantly, the breakthrough spurred Villa on to greater heights as Preston fell under a claret and blue cosh.

The passing by the home side was a joy to watch. One move started with Spencer and saw most of Villa's outfield players have a touch before Athersmith was sent away. Having patiently awaited an opening, keeping the ball away from any Preston boot, Villa caught their opponents out with a brilliant change of pace and Charlie raced clear. His rising shot was headed for the top of the net when Trainer spectacularly tipped the ball over for a corner. It was a brilliant move which had the crowd cheering wildly.

A free-kick following a Preston back handling the ball led to a goalmouth scramble during which Trainer saved no less than four shots as the ball pinged around his area. At the other end, a thunderous clash between Stephenson and Albert Evans saw both men temporarily leave the field for treatment. Evans suffered a nasty gash to his right eye in the challenge but he and his adversary were soon back in the thick of things.

The game evened out slightly as the half wore to a close. Trainer saved another Athersmith scorcher, then Crabtree headed clear Boyd's goal-bound shot. But two minutes from the break, Villa doubled their lead. Athersmith sprinted down the right and knocked over a cross. Devey, arriving late, met the ball with a perfectly directed header to score his, and his team's, second of the match.

Preston began the second period the brighter and Wilkes was called upon to make some acrobatic saves. Five minutes in from the re-start, North End reduced the deficit following a rare mistake from Howard Spencer. He miskicked the ball sending it into the danger area. Sadly, Ecclestone was in the right place at the right time and took his very simple chance .

Villa attacked immediately from the kick-off. Athersmith raced away and his cross caused panic in the North End defence before eventually being hoofed clear. Then, twice Campbell and once Smith saw cracking efforts stopped by the faultless Trainer.

Twenty minutes from time, Villa forced a corner. Wheldon swung it in just under the crossbar where a defender got a faint touch on the ball. This only succeeded in diverting the leather to Athersmith who found the net. Immediately after

this third goal, Wheldon was tripped as he was about to shoot. Match reports suggest it should have been a penalty but the referee only gave a free-kick. That turned out to be Villa's last meaningful attack of the match. Preston tried to get back into the game but, apart from a Boyd shot which hit the bar, the backs and halves did a fine job of saving Wilkes from being called into action. Villa thus won 3-1 and found themselves five points clear of their nearest rivals, Derby County, at the top of the table.

* * *

There was barely time to quaff a pint in the Old Crown and Cushion before the eleven who had defeated Preston joined Jimmy Whitehouse, Jeremiah Griffiths and John Cowan on a train to Blackpool. They were to stay at the seaside town's Station Hotel until the match at North End on the 27th. There was, as it turns out, no need to rush however, as the London and North-West Railway Company was beginning another long-standing tradition by running their trains some two hours late. And so it was a tired but happy Villa team who settled down for their first night in their temporary home. Four more days under the supervision of Lees and Grierson was purposed to get them spot on for the game which would lead the winners into the semi-finals of the FA Cup.

On Tuesday, the players had a Turkish bath which was followed up by a dip in the bitterly cold Irish Sea. He could be a cruel man could that Joe Grierson! Then it was time for a nice long walk to take in the bracing Lancashire sea air. In the evening, the players kept themselves amused by playing whist and having a singing session round the Hotel's piano. Fortunately, Jas Cowan refrained from joining in the latter. Mind you, the team were lucky that it was Grierson who coached them and not Brian Little. The modern managerial maestro banned card playing on away trips when he first took over at Villa Park! At least in 1897, the presence of a card table prevented Jas from flexing his vocal muscles.

The next day, the players had to work a little harder. Sprinting was the main exercise for the day's training sessions. To make it more bearable, Grierson arranged an 80 yard handicap. Athersmith gave the rest of the side starts of varying lengths. Jas received 2 yards, Crabtree 2½. Griffiths was handed a further couple whilst Smith and John Cowan started from the 5 yard mark. Then it was Evans, Spencer and Wilkes (6 each), Devey (7), Whitehouse (8), Wheldon (9), Campbell (10½), with slow-coach Reynolds receiving a massive 12½ yard lead over Charlie. The handicap was decided at the famous Raikes Hall Grounds and after the morning heats, Whitehouse and Campbell progressed to Thursday's final having beaten

Spencer and Smith respectively in the afternoon semi-finals.

The day of the eagerly-awaited final began with a bit of training with the ball. Then it was time for the serious business as Spencer claimed 3rd place in the sprints challenge after easily beating Smith. In the final, Whitehouse had a titanic struggle with John Campbell with the 'keeper just taking victory on the line. Athersmith and Jas Cowan suffered though, as their sprinting credentials were quizzed by the rest of the team.

Thursday evening saw an example of how Aston Villa players enjoyed celebrity status throughout the country. The manager of the Grand Theatre invited the team to watch a performance of The Geisha - and ensured that the local press and any potential ticket purchasers knew that the world famous Football Club's star names would be in attendance. The 'superstars' then spent their last day in Blackpool taking more sea-front walks and discussing plans for the slaughter of the Preston lambs.

The training camp had been a roaring success with the players in perfect mental and physical condition. As we shall see, they'd need to be. It wasn't all good news for the Villa, however. Word came down from Manchester that Bob Chatt would be out for the rest of the season. Mr. Whitehead had put Chatt's injured toe in a glass mould which would stay on for two months. Meanwhile, in Birmingham Jimmy Welford, who had been left out of the squad that travelled to Blackpool, was in trouble again. It was announced that he had been suspended until the end of March: "*. . .for neglect of training regulations and generally unsatisfactory conduct.*" Welford would never play a first-class match for Villa again.

* * *

Deepdale was abuzz. The enclosure had been enlarged to house an additional 3,000 spectators all keen to see if North End could stop Villa from getting a step closer to emulating their unique Double feat. In the dressing rooms, the home side prepared themselves in the knowledge that victory would mean a £2.10s bonus. The Villa players were on for £3 for the win. Back outside, 15,500 made their way through the turnstiles. 1,100 of them had taken advantage of the railway specials which got them from Birmingham and back again for 4 shillings (20p). A similar number came on other trips.

What the crowd were treated to was a typical full-throttle cup-tie. Throughout, the result could have gone either way. Preston made one change from the eleven who lost at Perry Barr with Pratt coming in for Ecclestone. The Villa, though, were

unchanged and looking super-fit after their efforts at Holt Fleet and Blackpool.

The visitors lost the toss and faced the wind and sun, but for the first ten minutes they crucified their hosts. The forwards were right on top of their game with, of course, Athersmith and Devey in mean form as the front-line zipped passes around the Deepdale pitch with deadly accuracy. Athersmith broke away and beat two men as he cut inside. He hit a great low shot which was destined for the bottom corner until Trainer stretched himself to tip the ball round the post. From Wheldon's corner, Athersmith put the ball into the net but the referee, Captain Simpson, spotted that the Villa man had used his hand.

Preston then woke up and came at Villa with some menacing rushes. The home backs and halves hustled the visiting forwards whose passes started to go astray. John Devey was the worst in this respect. In attack, the North End half-backs fed their wingers well as the balance tipped in their favour. Spencer, though, reigned supreme and Evans alongside him was playing perhaps his best game. One escape for the Villa had nothing to do with strong back play however. Pratt crashed in a shot which rebounded off the post to the feet of Henderson three yards out. With a completely open goal in front of him, the Preston forward somehow managed to sky the ball over. It was a miss of comical proportions but, as the half hour mark was reached, the gaffe was forgotten as a corner led to the home side taking the lead. From there to the interval, Villa were pegged back in their own half but the defence held firm.

The Villa attacked North End from the re-start and five minutes into the half, Steve Smith went on a marvellous run that took him past three challenges before he cut in from the left and hit a ferocious swerving shot which cannoned off the bar. Campbell was following up and slammed the ball home from the rebound to level matters.

It was all Villa now as they stretched the home defence every which way. Reynolds and Campbell went close and Smith wasted a fairly easy chance by firing over. But by far the best effort came from a resurgent John Devey. He carried the ball three quarters of the length of the pitch leaving numerous defenders in his wake. He shot across Trainer who could do nothing but watch as the ball skimmed off the outside of the far post. Shortly after this, as the excitement rose, the crowd surged forward and the barriers gave way. Fortunately there were no injuries and the game was not delayed but, just as the crowd could not contain themselves, so the ground could not contain the crowd.

Having had it all their own way since half time,

Villa spent the last ten minutes defending as Preston came at them. They never got a clear opening, however, and Wilkes was not called into serious action as an enthralling cup-tie ended in stalemate.

The game had attracted only the third largest gate of the four ties played that day but the £867.17s represented the largest receipts from quarter-final day. Obviously the biggest draws meant upping the admission prices. Elsewhere, Liverpool and Nottingham Forest also drew 1-1, but Everton defeated Blackburn while Newton Heath lost to Derby, both games recording 2-0 scorelines.

The Villa-Preston replay was set for the following Wednesday at Perry Barr (no '10-day notice' police rule in those days) which meant the scheduled Annual Charity Sports and Football Match held by Aston Villa was postponed. It was, for some reason, thought that the FA Cup was slightly more important. Before the match came round, an FA meeting verified a rule change. Half-time intervals were not to exceed five minutes except by permission of the referee. Obviously there was no need to allot time for commercial breaks nor expert analyses!

Wednesday 3rd March saw 12,000 fans converge on Wellington Road despite abysmal weather which threatened the match. The referee okayed the pitch and the same Villa line-up went head-to-head again with a North End side which showed just one change from Saturday. The encounter finished goal-less thanks once again to James Trainer in goal who was, according to reports: *"...brilliant in the extreme."* Villa undoubtedly had the better of the game but the forwards didn't shoot too well. Athersmith was man of the match and his shots were the chief source of Trainer's grief. Campbell too had a good game.

Pretty passing between Campbell and Wheldon gave the latter a great chance in the 1st minute but his left foot shot went wide from 15 yards out. Even before that, Athersmith and Devey worked an opening which Smith wasted with an off-target effort. Shortly after Wheldon's miss, Smith set up Devey who shot tamely at Trainer. Then Smith carried the ball through the Preston defence only to shoot directly into the arms of the grateful North End custodian. Reynolds fired wide following a free-kick and Wheldon and Crabtree both saw long-range efforts fly over. Crabtree did force Trainer to save at the expense of a corner but this too came to naught. All this had happened within the first 20 minutes.

Even when Preston spent ten minutes reduced to ten men owing to the injured Sanders receiving lengthy treatment, Villa could not score. Half an hour had passed and Wilkes had yet to touch the ball whilst Trainer had made at least a dozen saves. Shortly afterwards, the Villa 'keeper was reminded that he was at work. He had ages to set himself before holding a very tame long-range shot. He was twice called into action again before half-time.

The second half wasn't much different. Athersmith four times, Devey, Wheldon, Campbell and Crabtree all had good chances but poor shooting and breathtaking goalkeeping combined to keep the score-sheet blank. The closest the crowd came to seeing a goal was when Orr hit the post for Preston in one of only three shots the visitors managed in the second period, and Athersmith hit the bar with an incredible effort following one of his long, speedy runs.

So a second replay was needed. The eventual winners knew that they would face Liverpool in the semi-final as they had done what the Villa found impossible and scored a goal. It only needed one to account for Forest in the other replay. It was announced that the players would be taken to Buxton Hydro to prepare for the next North End encounter scheduled for Bramall Lane Sheffield on 10th March. Shooting practice was no doubt high on Joe Grierson's list of activities.

* * *

On 6th March, Villa got a much needed break from both the FA Cup and that infernal Preston 'keeper when they travelled to the Town Ground, home of Nottingham Forest. The attendance numbered 8,000 and they saw a Villa side minus the injured Steve Smith, with John Cowan returning.

In the first 15 minutes, Villa had marginally the better of the exchanges and sixty seconds before the quarter hour was reached, they managed something they had such difficulty in achieving against Preston: they found the net. Crabtree was the provider, floating in a delightful free-kick which Devey met with a powerful header to put his team a goal to the good. From then until half-time, it was a case of Forest attacking forcefully with Villa occasionally breaking out on dangerous counters.

The second half began with Villa still holding the advantage by a goal to nil. But four minutes in, Forest got back on level terms when their outside-right, Spencer, scored a beauty from a very tight angle. The Villa had yet to escape their half since the teams returned from the break.

On 53 minutes, the visitors finally worked an opening. Campbell carried the ball through the heart of the Forest defence. His shot was only partly cleared and John Cowan celebrated his return to the side by following up to regain the lead for Villa. Almost immediately though, Evans failed to deal with an innocuous looking cross. He could only direct the ball to Forest's Spencer who notched his second.

The home side started to tire and Devey took full advantage, again from a free-kick. Howard Spencer floated the ball in and there was the skipper in the right place at the right time. The goal meant Devey was now Villa's leading scorer in the League with 13 to his credit. From here on in it was all Villa as the Pets outclassed Forest. Close on the call of time, Wheldon met an Athersmith corner with a spectacular over-head kick which propelled the ball at a rate of knots into the top corner of the net. The Villa triumphed 4-2 to set themselves up nicely for the next instalment of their mammoth FA Cup quarter-final.

Campbell was the star forward despite not getting on the score-sheet. Crabtree shone in the half-back line but Reynolds played badly and Howard Spencer often had to rescue his side following mistakes by Baldy. Still, everyone is allowed a bad day at the office and it was rare that Reynolds suffered one. Meanwhile, back at Perry Barr, the reserves were held 1-1 by Brierly Hill Alliance in a game which saw Villa give an outing to seven trialists. None of them made the grade!

* * *

Bramall Lane was a famous cricket enclosure a century ago, as well as being the home of Sheffield United. It was one of the premier grounds in England, hence it was chosen as the venue for many games requiring a neutral stage. It was here that Villa and Preston would finally sort out their epic Cup-tie before 22,000 fans. Having had four away matches in the past month, Villa's travelling support was obviously feeling the effects in their wallets. Only 600 of them made the trip to Yorkshire and, with most of the 'neutrals' in the crowd favouring Preston as the perceived underdogs, the Lancastrians enjoyed the greater vocal support.

Preston did not have the funds to send their players to a training camp, unlike the Villa who had packed the squad off to Buxton Hydro from where they returned looking fit and healthy. North End had not played since the first replay but stories had circulated that four-fifths of their forward line were out with heavy colds. One of them, centre-forward Stephenson, was also said to be feeling the effects of the heavy challenges he received at Perry Barr. As things turned out, however, Preston fielded their strongest eleven. The Villa Committee decided to keep John Cowan on the extreme left rather than reinstate a recovered Steve Smith.

Villa began with the wind in their favour and

had the best of the opening exchanges. But, and this should come as no surprise, James Trainer pulled off a string of first-class saves to deny the Brummies again and again. That was until the 37th minute when, if one takes into account the game at Perry Barr, over two hours of incessant Villa pressure was rewarded. Wheldon completed a jinking run with a centre which deceived Trainer and whipped across the face of the goal. Athersmith raced in at the far post and headed into the unguarded net for the only score of the half.

Shortly after the break, a lovely passing move ended with Wheldon again providing a cross which Campbell met and neatly slipped past Trainer. From then, in the words of the *Birmingham Daily Post*. " . . . the crowd witnessed some of the fiercest and fastest football ever seen on an Association field."

Preston hurled themselves at Villa. Only a minute after Campbell's strike, they had pulled one back. They carried on the momentum and came close to drawing level on a couple of occasions But the Villa backs stayed solid against North End's pressure tactics and gradually the Villa pulled themselves back into the match with their precise, methodical passing. Twice John Cowan beat Trainer but the first was called offside and the second penalised for a premature charge on the 'keeper. No doubt Villa fans would have said Trainer deserved it having frustrated them so often. On the other wing, Athersmith showed some clever footwork to evade two challenges and again beat Trainer, this time for a legitimate score. The play then switched back and forth as Preston piled forward and left gaps at the back. Their tactics appeared to be working when they pulled one back but Villa held out to progress to the semi's courtesy of a 3-2 victory.

The game was played at a terrific pace throughout yet the skill level shown by both sides was incredibly high. Spencer was a rock at the back. Crabtree the pick of the halves. Reynold's aerial power did much to counter Preston's rushes while the Villa forwards played out of their skins, their passing towards the close being absolutely mesmeric.

Finally, another word about James Trainer - a survivor of Preston's 1889 Double winning team. He, and he alone, caused the tie to go on for 270 minutes. The Villa still had to play Preston in an away League fixture, but until 26th April Villa's forwards could sleep soundly in their beds without the nightmare image of a 'keeper who had frustrated their best efforts on so many occasions. It is unlikely that any crowd in any era have witnessed such grand custodianship as that displayed by the North End man at Perry Barr in the first replay.

An incredibly congested fixture list had been negotiated by the Villa and they had come through it unscathed. It is apt that they should have had such a titanic struggle with the only club to have completed the Double. When Preston ended their great 1888/9 season, they earned the tag 'The Invincibles'. Aston Villa too were becoming a fearsome adversary for the rest of football. Following on from the nightmare start to the year, they had put together an unbeaten run of ten League and Cup games and were getting better and better.

It wasn't just the results that made Villa great though. The press raved about their style, one paper commenting: *"Few teams play anything near as well."* It seemed other teams had to hope they caught the Pets on an off day because otherwise they were unstoppable.

The FA Cup had dominated a six week period, but Villa had performed well in the League and still sat proudly atop Division One, five points clear of the struggle for second spot:

		pld	home					away					g.av	pts
			w	d	l	f	a	w	d	l	f	a		
1	Aston Villa	24	7	2	2	22	14	9	2	2	34	21	1.60	36
2	Derby	24	10	1	2	43	19	4	2	5	18	20	1.56	31
3	Sheff U	25	5	4	4	21	14	5	6	1	17	11	1.52	30
4	Liverpool	26	7	4	1	22	6	5	2	7	21	28	1.26	30
5	Preston	22	7	3	1	31	17	2	5	4	16	17	1.38	26
6	Sheff W	25	7	4	2	24	11	1	6	5	10	20	1.10	26
7	Bolton	22	5	2	2	16	10	5	3	5	16	15	1.28	25
8	Everton	23	6	1	4	30	19	5	2	5	18	21	1.20	25
9	W Brom	25	6	2	6	15	16	3	3	5	12	26	0.64	23
10	N Forest	24	7	2	3	26	14	1	3	8	12	28	0.90	21
11	Bury	22	4	4	2	17	13	2	5	5	12	23	0.81	21
12	Blackburn	25	7	1	6	25	24	2	2	7	5	30	0.56	21
13	Stoke	24	5	3	3	24	17	3	0	10	17	38	0.75	19
14	Sunderland	27	4	5	5	19	19	2	2	9	11	25	0.68	19
15	Wolves	24	4	4	5	20	14	2	2	7	12	20	0.94	18
16	Burnley	24	3	5	4	18	19	1	2	9	15	30	0.67	15

We end this section with non-Villa news. Blackburn, who had spent most of the campaign in the bottom half, found themselves the victim of the Victorian equivalent of 'manager poaching'. For twelve years, Mr. T.B. Mitchell had been Rovers' secretary. Then, he resigned owing, apparently, to irreconcilable differences with the Committee over training methods. Mr. Mitchell turned up in London shortly after his spat at Blackburn. He accepted the post of secretary and team manager at Woolwich Arsenal where he was being paid a much larger salary that he received up North. Little did those 19th Century football men know how common such stories would become!

Chapter Eight

Forward To Victory
Centre And Left-side Forwards

If the half-backs were the unsung heroes of the team, then Steve Smith, John Cowan, John Campbell and Fred Wheldon were the unsung heroes of the forward line. The reason for this was that the press filled most of their column inches raving about the right-wing of Athersmith and Devey. This wasn't surprising as these two possessed an eye-catching brilliance which tended to blind observers to the skills of others. Yet the rest of the forward line was also packed with talent and all of them would have walked into any other team.

In the outside-left position, Villa had the choice of two men of very similar style. John Cowan we shall come to, but first the ever-alert Steve Smith. Watch the best teams from any era and one will see that they all have a player who, when a shot goes in on goal, will follow it up. Every season, these players will supplement their side's 'goals for' column by knocking in a few rebounds. Steve Smith did that for Villa throughout the 1890's. Opposition 'keepers had to hold on to shots because, if they let the ball run loose, there would be the moustachioed winger waiting to pounce.

Steve's life began in the same year as Aston Villa's: 1874. Born near Hednesford he soon became quite a star of local football where his speed and exquisite skill put him head and shoulders above his contemporaries. But his sporting activities had to take a back seat to his day job at

Steve Smith

Cannock & Rugeley Colliery.

In the summer of 1893, Smith was down the pit working as a haulage-machine operator when he received a visitor. The one and only Fred Rinder had gone underground armed with a League form for Smith to sign. Steve was a coal miner when he went to work that morning. When he next saw daylight he was a professional footballer and future England International.

On 28th October of the same year, he took to the Perry Barr pitch as Aston Villa entertained Burnley. Cutting in from the left-wing, he scored Villa's first in a 4-0 victory to cap a marvellous debut. That 1893/4 season saw him make 15 appearances for the Pets but, more importantly, he picked up his first of five Championship medals. The following year he missed just four games and occasionally turned out at inside-left and inside-right before he made his one appearance in a Cup Final as Villa beat West Brom at Crystal Palace. He rounded off a great campaign by scoring against Scotland when winning his solitary England cap, and played against the Scottish League.

During those first two years in professional football, Smith was helped, no doubt, by the presence of the great Dennis Hodgetts alongside him. Just as Albert Evans learned quickly with the assistance of Crabtree, Jas Cowan and Howard Spencer, so Villa's raw left-wing recruit settled in beautifully thanks to the legend he shared the flank with.

Smith was a great favourite with the Villa fans. While he was not as fast as Charlie Athersmith (who was?) he still had enough pace to trouble defenders. He could also use both feet equally well and his two-footed trickery bemused many a back. But his most useful attribute was his stamina. Steve possessed exceptionally strong legs which could keep going when others were floundering around him

Out for much of the '95/6 season, although he still played enough games to pick up a Championship medal, Smith found a threat to his position with the purchase of Jas Cowan's brother, John The battle between the two lasted through the Double year before Cowan looked to have made the position his own in '97/8. Smith had other ideas though and came back stronger than ever as the Villa won a fourth League title in 1899.

He continued to star for the side until the Autumn of 1901, occasionally turning out in the outside-right position when injury depleted the squad But his ninth season with the Club never really got under way and he was transferred to Portsmouth where, at the end of the season, he added a Southern League Championship medal to his haul of honours.

Following five seasons in Hampshire, he took the post of player-manager at New Brompton, the club that became Gillingham FC. There he lasted just two years before he retired from the game and moved back to Portsmouth to open his own business. At the age of 61, having moved to Oxfordshire, this hugely under-rated footballer died

Perhaps the biggest regret Smith had was his lack of England appearances. He was definitely International class yet he won only one cap. He would have doubled that amount in 1897 had he been fit to line-up against Wales, but if the England selectors had anything about them they would have made Steve a regular

But, as has already been mentioned, he wasn't always a regular in the Villa side owing to another man who didn't receive the credit he was due.

* * *

John Cowan claimed he always wanted to play for the Villa. His feelings for the Club were strengthened by his brother's presence in the team. It was 1895 that John's dream came true. Having already played for Preston he was plying his trade at Glasgow Rangers when the call came from Perry Barr. He was an instant hit in Brum. His chance came early when Steve Smith picked up an injury and Cowan notched up 26 starts in his first season with Aston Villa.

He shared many attributes with his left-wing competitor, not least his versatility. In that '95/6 season he turned out in all the forward positions bar the centre. Like the whole Villa team, Cowan could use both feet and it doesn't take much imagination to work out what these greats would have thought about today's highly paid one-footed superstars.

Smith and Cowan had comparable speed and a vast array of tricks which all great wingers need to possess. The other skill which they were required to have was the ability to cross a ball accurately. There was no 'hit and hope' centres at the Villa as Joe Grierson had his wide men spend-

John Cowan

ing hours knocking balls into the middle. Hence it was very rare that a cross went astray.

Where John Cowan had an edge over the other flank players was in his eye for goal. He regularly piled in with stunningly accurate shots. He netted 28 times in his 74 appearances for the Villa giving him a far better goals per game ratio than any other wingers of the day.

His greatest moment undoubtedly came when he was selected for the Villa team which contested the FA Cup Final of 1897. In that match, like so many he played in, his cross-field balls to Charlie Athersmith were a prominent feature while his control of return balls from the right-wing was excellent. Again, Joe Grierson's training sessions had much to do with this.

It was 1899 when Cowan left the club he adored. Many Scottish footballers returned north of the Border in the late '90's, prompted by the International selectors' reluctance to pick English based players. John Cowan never really had any desire to follow the exodus, but his future didn't look too bright at Villa so he took up an offer to play in Dundee. Much is made of the benefit of having local-born players in football teams because they possess a deeper love for the club than do outsiders, but there can't be too many Brummies who held a greater depth of feeling for Aston Villa than did John Cowan.

* * *

William McGregor wrote the following about the Class of '96/7: *"If there was a man... who made the side more than another, that man was John Campbell. The Villa had had no centre since Archie Hunter was compelled by failing health to give up the game. Centres are hard to procure, and the Villa could not get one. Then they intro-duced John Campbell, and he filled the position perfectly. He was the one man in the football world who was suited to Aston Villa's methods, and when he left them for Celtic the club went down*

John Campbell

materially..."

Two seasons John Campbell was at Villa - only two seasons. Just as Peter Withe was the last piece in Ron Saunders' Championship jigsaw, so Campbell was the man who lifted the Villa from the level of 'great' to a plateau of perfection. It wasn't easy getting him and it was a constant battle to keep him. He wasn't always appreciated by fans and experts alike, indeed by anyone who couldn't grasp the concept that a centre forward could be more than a battering ram. But the team knew what he gave to them. The Committee understood how vital he was. The Double was his and their reward.

Campbell was a natural born footballer. Just as he made his first appearance in the world in Glasgow, the football Gods must have looked upon the planet and decided there wasn't enough talent about. With that thought, they espied the infant John and injected his genes with more ability than most professionals of any era could possibly dream of.

That was 1871. Twenty years on, Celtic spot-ted the awesome talent scoring hatfuls of goals for the local Benburb club, and they grabbed him. They never wanted to let him go and, when they lost him, they did everything in their power to get him back

Like all Scottish forwards, Campbell was strong and brave. He would put his head in where others would fear to venture unless they were heavily armed. He possessed great balance which allowed

him to hold off challenges and, when required, bundle his way through defenders and goalkeep-ers. But there was much more to his game than mere brawn for Johnny was that rarest of crea-tures: a thinking centre forward, and this more than made up for his lack of natural speed.

First off, he had great close control which, when coupled with his balance, made him a drib-bler par excellence. He was one of those players who could, with a moment of sheer individualistic brilliance, turn a game. It was vital that his marker didn't give Campbell a yard of space because he would exploit it every time and if he got the ball under control and ran at the opposition, the best they could hope to do was send him into a cul de sac because they weren't going to win the ball off him.

Even against the tightest markers, though, Campbell would create his own space. His favourite trick was to move to make a forward run, taking the defender with him, then check back and drop deep. If the halves were doing their job, they would lay a pass to Johnny who was a master at shielding the ball and holding up play to give oth-ers a chance to support. More often than not in this situation, Campbell would sweep the ball out to the wing and turn his marker, getting that all-important couple of yards of space as he headed for the goal-mouth to receive a return from the flanks.

On top of this ability to set up opportunities for his side, he was also a formidable scorer. In just 63 games for Aston Villa, he netted 43 times, one of those goals earning him a permanent place in Villa history as we shall shortly find out. His left foot was the most feared weapon in football and his right was better than most naturally right-sided players possessed. And he could score from any-where, be it a 30 yard scorcher or a poached tap-in from near the goal line.

In 1895, Villa made a move for Campbell. The Club had been knocked back by Celtic a number of times before, but Campbell thought it was the right time to fulfil his ambition to play in England. The move wasn't entirely good news for him. Having already won two Scotland caps in 1893, he was tipped to become the regular centre for his country. But, as has already been noted, the selec-tors frowned upon English clubs poaching the best tartan talent and Campbell didn't play for his coun-try until he returned to his native land, whereafter he appeared in a further 10 internationals.

In his first season at Perry Barr, he averaged a goal a game in the League which kept the crowd happy. But they seemed to be less impressed in the Double year. This was partly due to the fact that Campbell played better in away games in '96/7 than in front of his own supporters. Teams were less inclined to attack at Wellington Road so Johnny suffered closer attention than on Villa's travels.

Another reason for him having his critics was that centre forwards were supposed to 'put themselves about' and crash into 'keepers at every opportunity. All the pretty stuff was for the other forwards. The 'thuglovers' in the crowd could not see the point of a centre forward dropping into midfield to receive the ball. But it doesn't take much to see Campbell's value to the Villa. Even though he averaged less than a goal every two League games in '96/7, Villa finished the season as top scorers. That was, in no small measure, due to Campbell's ability to bring the best out of his fellow forwards.

In the summer of 1896, Celtic tried desperately to get Campbell to 'come home'. If he'd have gone, quite simply, Villa would not have done the Double. A year later, Celtic finally persuaded him to return. They wanted him so badly that he was paid a £70 signing-on fee by the Glasgow club, as against the £30 Jimmy Welford received when signing at the same time as Campbell.

The success continued in Scotland. He already had one Scottish Championship medal from 1892 and added others in 1899 and 1900, plus a Scottish Cup winners medal in 1898. Johnny was one of the players who helped the injured at the Ibrox disaster in 1902 when a stand collapsed during the Scotland versus England match. A year later, he moved to Third Lanark and won another title.

He retired from the game in 1906 and lived in his native land until the end of 1947 when he died aged 76. He had been the finest centre forward of his day and one of the most complete players of any era. The more ignorant sections of the Villa crowd may not always have understood what Campbell was doing, but he earned the respect of the Lions' faithful who over the generations have come to revere the 'Number 9' shirt. And John Campbell was every bit as worthy an occupant of that shirt as Hunter, Hampton, Waring, Broome, Edwards, Ford, Hitchens, Hateley, Gray and Withe.

* * *

That just leaves 'Diamond' as Fred Wheldon was known to football fans the country over. He was born in Langley Green in 1871, the youngest of ten children. He began his career at Langley Green Vics from where, at the tender age of 19, Small Heath signed him up. Having been a member of their 1893 Division Two winning team, he quickly became a crowd favourite at Coventry Road and was regarded as one of the best for-

Fred Wheldon

wards in the land.

It became obvious, however, that he was stagnating in the poor Small Heath side. By 1896, when they were relegated, he was far and away their best player but often found himself isolated on the left-wing. Opposing teams knew that by neutralising the threat of Fred, they neutralised the whole team. This prompted the *Birmingham Daily Post* to upset the Small Heath Committee (something they seemed to do regularly) by commenting in the summer of 1896:

"In a club like the Villa, for instance, we think Wheldon would be very prominent, for the opposing half-backs and backs could not pay him that close attention that they have done in the last two seasons."

Within a few weeks of that quote appearing, Wheldon moved to Villa for a world record transfer fee. Villa paid £100 down and guaranteed £250 from the proceeds of a friendly match, plus half of any excess.

The move did wonders for Fred's game. No longer was the whole attacking responsibility carried on his shoulders. In the nicest possible way, he looked ordinary in the Villa front rank because he was playing alongside the best in the world. The proof of Wheldon's brilliance, however, was that he never once looked out of place in such glorious company.

Revelling in the additional space he was granted by defenders, who were just as worried about Wheldon's colleagues as they were with the man himself, Fred would murder backs with his close control. The Villa were blessed with several class dribblers and Wheldon was one of the best. Like John Campbell, he didn't possess lightning speed but he didn't really need it. He formed a great understanding with both Steve Smith and John Cowan as he slotted into his favoured inside-left role, although Wheldon was another who could play in any of the forward positions.

'Diamond' was one of Villa's army of all-round sportsmen. He qualified for Worcestershire at cricket and scored three centuries as he notched up a career total of nearly 5,000 runs for the County. In addition, he took nearly 100 catches behind the stumps.

But football was always his number one game. In 138 appearances for the Villans, he scored 74 times and picked up three Championship gongs and one FA Cup medal. His goals were especially valuable to the Club in the '97/8 season as they struggled to compensate for the loss of John Campbell. But in the Double year, he and John Devey capitalised on the opportunities presented to them by defenders who expected Villa's main attacking threat to be the centre forward.

The summer of 1900 saw Wheldon depart Villa Park and take the short trip to West Bromwich Albion. A disappointing season ended with the Baggies being relegated and Fred moved on to Queen's Park Rangers. A year later and he was on his travels again, this time to Portsmouth where he stayed for three years, linking up once more with Steve Smith. Then he gradually made his way back to the West Midlands. Worcester City benefited from Wheldon's services in the 1905/6 campaign before a year at Coventry proved to be his last in football.

Fred added representative honours to his various achievements at club level. We already know about his hat-trick against the Irish on his England debut. In 1898 he played in all three Home Internationals. He also represented the League four times, playing against the Irish and Scottish Leagues in 1894 and repeating the feat in 1898. After his glittering career came to an end, Fred lived in Worcestershire until his death in 1924 aged 52. A genuine Villa great - even if he did once play for Small Heath!

* * *

The Villa forward line was arguably the best ever assembled in the entire 'W' era. Every one of the front players had incredible skill, great tactical awareness, perfect control, an astounding level of versatility and, despite the odd lapse, a great eye for goal. Much of Villa's success in the pre First World War years can be put down to the fact that their forwards were so good that they each demanded to be given special attention by opposing defences. But if any of them were singled out as the danger-man, there were four others who would prove equally as dangerous. At times, they were simply unstoppable.

Chapter Nine

Taking The North-West Passage To London

In 1897 there was no place for footballers who claimed the season was too long and the fixture list too congested. If there was a game to be played, you played it! Tiredness was about as acceptable an excuse for a poor performance as saying that one couldn't see team-mates because of the colour of the their shirts.

Anyway, Villa players didn't have time for tiredness as, three days after defeating Preston, they had to entertain Liverpool. Once again, the Perry Barr faithful had a chance to weigh up forthcoming Cup opposition and the game was billed as a dress rehearsal for the semi-final scheduled for seven days later. What they saw would hardly put the Claret & Blue Army in good cheer.

Nearly 20,000 supporters watched a much changed Liverpool team take the field with no less than three of their front-line out. Included in their absentees was Beckton who was, it seems, determined not to play at Perry Barr. Wilkie was also missing from his usual left-back berth. Villa, on the other hand paraded the same outfield ten but replaced Wilkes with Whitehouse.

The pitch was perfect. There was very little wind. Only once during the game did the sun emerge to dazzle the players. The conditions were perfect for a game between two of the best teams in the world. And the match was exceedingly - and inexplicably - poor.

Liverpool attacked the Wellington Road end in the first half and enjoyed all the territorial advantage, their forwards playing short, sharp passes in a near perfect copy of the Villa style. Allan in the centre played very well, bringing the wings into play and testing Whitehouse more than once. The visitors' pressure eventually told when, following a free-kick and a goal-mouth melee, they found the Villa net. But the referee had already blown his whistle for a foul on a Liverpool player. Rather than a goal, the Merseysiders only got another free-kick which Reynolds cleared easily.

The first-half had seen Storer in the Liverpool goal have little to do while Whitehouse did a passable impression of Trainer of Preston. The Villa defence had been steady though, as this quote shows: *"The imperturbable Spencer was always in*

the place to do the right thing in the right way." Evans, meanwhile, was his usual dogged self.

The second half saw Villa's forwards belatedly come into the game. But on 55 minutes Crabtree hobbled off having slipped and badly strained his leg. He didn't reappear. Now reduced to ten men, Villa raised their game and they repeatedly attacked their opponents. Reynolds, Devey and Wheldon brought saves out of Storer, and Goldie almost gifted Villa an own goal. John Cowan then ended a beautifully worked left-wing move with a close-range effort which seemed certain to go in. Dunlop hooked the ball away as it brushed the goal-line. Villa claimed a goal but their protests were to no avail.

As Villa pushed forward, they left gaps at the back. One Liverpool break away saw Spencer and Whitehouse isolated against four forwards but, thanks to the attackers' ineptitude rather than good defence, the chance went begging.

The game ended goal-less, the two rearguards coming out with most credit. Of the Villa front five, only Campbell performed well. The real talking point about the match was the performance of the man with the whistle, Mr. J West, who annoyed the crowd with his over-officious handling of the game. And he didn't have a plethora of FIFA directives to use as an excuse for his whistle-happy show!

Press reports show how forgettable the game was. One was headed: *" The failure of Aston Villa"* and stated: *"The Villa were giving one of those inert displays which they seem to have specially reserved for the Perry Barr crowd during the present season."* Not good then?

* * *

As was becoming increasingly common, Villa disappeared off to a training camp. This time, Buxton Hydro was the setting for the team's final preparation for the Cup semi against Liverpool. With Bramall Lane on their minds, the ten who finished Saturday's League game along with Griffiths, Burton, Smith and Wilkes were being put through their paces by Joe Grierson, all under the ever-watchful eye of James Lees. Crabtree was absent having been sent to Manchester to receive treatment on his thigh strain.

The first part of the week at Buxton saw outdoor work limited by the weather, but later on the squad managed to get in some practice with the ball. Otherwise, Grierson got them doing weight-training, skipping, sprinting and walking to get his charges into perfect condition. Crabtree, it was announced, would not play at Bramall Lane. He broke down during fitness tests in Manchester and his place in the side would be taken by Griffiths.

Liverpool, meanwhile, prepared themselves at Freshfield and, having secured a draw at Wellington Road, were understandably confident of victory. But the Villa were hardly lacking in self-belief, predicting that they would line-up against Derby in the Final.

On Saturday 20th March, 30,000 people paid a collective £917. 7s. 1d. to watch a very one-sided semi-final. The Bramall Lane crowd, which included over 10,000 Villa fans, did not see a great game by any means, but then semi-finals are about winning rather than entertaining.

The first half was a bit of a scramble. Nerves played a big part on both sides and one or two incidents saw tempers become frayed. Liverpool played with great dash but little science which was surprising after their classy demonstration at Perry Barr. Bradshaw was the exception though, as he played with skill and caused the Villa defence a few problems.

But it was at the other end that the backs really had their work cut out. Devey and Athersmith were on top form and the crosses from the rightwing induced panic in the Liverpool goal-mouth. It was a ball from the right, this time a Howard Spencer free-kick, which led to Villa taking the lead in the 35th minute. John Cowan met the cross beautifully with his left instep, screwing the leather into the far corner. It was an unstoppable shot which turned out to be the difference between the sides at the interval for, while Liverpool strove to equalise, the Villa backs and halves were always in control.

The start of the second half found Liverpool matching Aston Villa for a while, but when the latter stepped up a gear they began to outclass their adversaries in stunning style. The Villa forwards worked perfectly as a unit and carried the ball through the Reds defence with consummate ease. Campbell and Wheldon thumped shots past Storer only to see them hit the post as Villa continued to dominate. Reward for that pressure came when Athersmith sent in a corner which Wheldon headed in for 2-0.

Liverpool were a beaten combination. They tried to get back into it but simply couldn't break the Villa down. Bradshaw and Spencer had a great battle but Howard eventually won it and was top candidate for a man of the match title that could have gone to anyone in claret and blue. He was supreme and in a game where many strong and illegal challenges flew in, Howard timed everything to perfection. As the *Birmingham Daily Post* reported: *"Whatever he did was open and above board and the crowd greatly appreciated his display."*

The Villa set about outplaying Liverpool and went further ahead with a stunning goal. Athersmith set off from the halfway line at an incredible pace. Dunlop attempted the impossible when he tried to tackle Charlie, but Villa's winger beat the back with a lovely change of direction and crashed a right foot shot into the net. Storer barely saw the ball let alone had chance to save it.

Now 3-0 up, Villa sat back and let Liverpool attack, but they could not get close enough in to trouble Whitehouse, such was the dominance shown by Villa's backs. Not even a returned Beckton could do much. He had been hit in the face with the ball in the opening minutes and seemed to lack much stomach for a fight after that. The best team won and each of the men who took the Club to the Final deserved immense praise for their faultless performance.

Whitehouse did everything that was expected of him but he was very well protected. Spencer, as we know, was pure perfection. Evans played out of his skin, his performance being all the more creditable when one considers he didn't have the security of Crabtree ahead of him. Reynolds supplied the forwards well and Jas was a rock past which nothing and no one went. Jeremiah Griffiths had the look of a man who plays in semi-finals every week rather than the Birmingham and District League.

Up front, John Cowan used a combination of speed, skill and brilliant shooting to terrorise Liverpool. Wheldon was below par but still troubled Storer on a number of occasions and had one or two useful runs. Campbell had no joy in front of goal but his ability to hold up play and to find his team-mates with stunningly accurate balls did much to ensure victory. Devey dribbled brilliantly and didn't send a single pass astray all game. And Charlie was, well, Charlie! The best footballer in the world.

The press had an uncomfortable moment during the match. An exciting piece of play had the journalists leaning so far forward that the bench they were sitting on gave way sending twenty of the Fourth Estate's finest tumbling.

Over at Stoke, a similar sized crowd to the one

at Bramall Lane paid £1,200 to see Everton defeat Derby in the other semi-final. The first half ended goal-less but also saw County reduced to ten men when Leiper hobbled out of the action. Derby seemed to get better after that but Everton were always the stronger side. The final score was deceptively close, but two goals from Hartley and one from Milward gave Everton the edge by 3 to 2.

The results in the two games led the press to conclude: *"Villa and Everton should be the best final tie that has taken place for many years and doubtless, if the weather is fine, will command a record gate."*

* * *

The victorious Villa squad returned to Buxton after the conquest of Liverpool and remained there until Monday 22nd March when they came home to Brum for the League match against Bolton Wanderers. It had not been confirmed at the time that this match would prove to be the last first-team game played at Wellington Road. If it had been known, more than the 8,000 who turned up would have been there to bid farewell to the famous enclosure which had seen so many glorious Villa triumphs. The team that represented the world's finest football club on that historic day showed two changes to the eleven that had won the Cup semi-final 48 hours earlier:

Wilkes, Spencer, Evans, Reynolds, Jas Cowan, Griffiths, Athersmith, Devey, Campbell, Wheldon, Smith.

For once, that tired old cliche: *"It was a game of two halves"* is most appropriate. For an hour it looked like being an inadequate end to a glorious era. But then, just as when Liverpool visited Villa Park on the last day of the famous Holte End terrace 97 years later, the home team suddenly produced a performance worthy of the occasion.

In the first half Bolton, minus McGeachan and Thomson, were excellent and there was no sign of what was to come. The visitors won the toss and played downhill with the wind, but the first attack saw Villa look menacing. Smith beat three men before slipping a pass inside to Wheldon whose shot went narrowly over the bar. Wheldon himself then went it alone and, like his wing partner before him, left a trio of defenders in his wake but could not find a shot to match the run.

The promise of those opening few minutes was not fulfiled and it was Bolton who took control of the game. For long periods they pushed Villa back, yet they failed to threaten Wilkes to any great extent. That was except for one incident which Howard Spencer would be keen to forget. 17 minutes had elapsed when he went to clear an innocu-

ous looking cross. But Howard slipped and missed his kick completely, leaving Jack with the easy task of slipping the ball into the net.

Until then, despite Wanderers' territorial superiority, it was the Villa who had looked more dangerous in front of goal. But the strike gave Bolton a lift and they pressed Villa hard. When the home side did break, it was through Wheldon and Smith that they caused the most panic in the Bolton defence. Both of them combined well and each had efforts which severely tested Sutcliffe in goal. Bolton themselves kept Wilkes busy but it was Athersmith who found himself with the easiest chance of the half. With an open goal in front of him, Charlie managed to get under the ball and send it over, a move which didn't please the crowd.

Both 'keepers were being worked hard as play swung from end to end and it was Wilkes who again had to retrieve the ball from his goal on 40 minutes when Jack scored his second with a well struck low shot. On the stroke of half-time, Reynolds nearly got Villa off the mark when he let fly from 25 yards only to see the ball canon off the upright. Halfway through this landmark match, Bolton led 2-0 and Wellington Road was not a happy place to be for Villa fans.

The second half started in heavy rain and the Villa attacked from the off. Less than a minute after the re-start, Smith hit a right-foot shot which Sutcliffe could only half stop. The ball crossed the line and rolled out but, despite Villa's protests, the referee said no goal. The play then swung from end to end up to the hour mark when a great transformation came over the Villa team and, consequently, the match itself.

On 62 minutes, Campbell received the ball from Jas Cowan and swept a pass out to Athersmith. Both Summerville and Scott misread the path of the ball completely, leaving the Villa winger to run in close and beat Sutcliffe. From here to the end it was all Villa.

Two further attacks produced no return before Reynolds took aim from long-range once more. This time, only the net stopped his thunderbolt from leaving the ground and, such was the power behind the shot, exiting the entire Perry Barr district. A glorious goal had brought Aston Villa level and such was their dominance that it was only a matter of time before they took the lead. The beleaguered Bolton backs could only stand and watch as first Wheldon headed over and then Athersmith sent in a shot which Sutcliffe painfully turned away. Smith went close before he sent over a cross which Campbell met on the volley to give Villa the lead.

When Wheldon made it four on 72 minutes,

Villa had produced 10 minutes of awesome foot-ball which turned a two goal deficit into a two goal lead. And they weren't finished. Athersmith centred to Wheldon whose shot forced a shell-shocked Sutcliffe into an acrobatic save. The same pair combined again for Wheldon to coolly stop the ball five yards out before tapping it past the poor 'keep-er in the afternoon's cheekiest goal. Then Wheldon turned provider when his corner a minute from time was headed in by Devey.

The last big crowd at Perry Barr had seen a match which mirrored the entire history of Aston Villa Football Club, a history which can be summed up in the following phrase: "Never do it the easy way when you can make life difficult for yourself." Throughout its lifespan, Aston Villa have produced teams which have taken inconsistency to unprecedented heights. They are easily the most unpredictable club in the world. 2-0 down after an hour against Bolton, a team they should have beaten easily. Then, just as it seemed that they would once again be embarrassed by inferior opposition, they produced the kind of football which could only come from the Villa. They like to give their fans the odd heart attack do Aston Villa but, when things are going badly, there is some unquantifiable quality which pulls them through adversity. It was like that in 1897. It has been like that from 1874 to the present day. It will ever be like that. Against Bolton, the great Villa Gods had looked down on Wellington Road and seen their side in trouble. So, through divine intervention, they came to the rescue of the team and ensured that the passing of Perry Barr would be a joyous, if tearful, occasion.

* * *

Frank Burton replaced Griffiths in the Villa line-up which travelled to Burnden Park to contest the return fixture with Bolton on 27th March. That is because the latter had picked up an injury at the Perry Barr meeting of the two teams five days ear-lier. There were two other changes: in goal where Whitehouse returned, and on the left-wing which saw John Cowan replace Steve Smith. Griffiths and Jimmy Crabtree watched the game from the stands having come over from Manchester where they were being treated. It is debatable whether or not John Reynolds wanted to see Crabtree recover as 'Baldy' was in line to take Jimmy's place in the England team to face Wales if his injury hadn't cleared up in time.

The 7,000 who paid their entrance money was a 1,000% rise on Burnden Park's lowest ever gate of 700 who watched the home team defeat Villa in November 1893. But the 1897 crowd nearly didn't see any football at all. The match had been due to start at 3:30 but the Villa team had been told 4pm was kick-off time. Fortunately, the late-arriving Lions were allowed to play as the ref accepted their explanation.

In a hard game played on heavy ground and in a strong wind, plenty of fouls were conceded as the backs and halves enjoyed dominance over the forwards. Passes regularly went astray but individ-ual skill was evident in flashes. Villa controlled matters without ever stamping complete authority over the Wanderers and chose to take things easy in the second half.

In the opening 45 minutes, with the help of the wind, Villa opened up a two-goal lead. Wheldon was first on the score-sheet with a goal following an Athersmith cross. Then, with four minutes to go to the interval, Spencer floated in a free-kick from which Devey powerfully headed home. After the break, Villa were content to soak up Bolton pres-sure and counter menacingly, but the home side pulled one back on the hour through McGeachan.

Villa's shooting was not as it could have been, but although Bolton enjoyed greater possession in the second half it was Sutcliffe who was the busier 'keeper by a long way. Spencer was invincible at the back while alongside him, Evans had another blinder. He was getting better with every match and each new experience seemed noticeably to increase his confidence. Burton worked hard while Reynolds was masterful throughout although Jas Cowan shone above the 21 other players on show. The right-wing, especially Athersmith, played well but the forwards never really got their flowing game going. They didn't need to.

Back at Perry Barr, even though the enclosure was living on borrowed time, Walsall upset the odds to beat Wolves 2-1 in the Birmingham Senior Cup Final. A couple more reserve matches would be played at Wellington Road in a low-key end to twenty-one glorious years of football on the site.

Elsewhere, the League saw a shock result when Burnley won their second away match of the season (their first being at the Villa of course) by inflicting only the second home defeat of the cam-paign on Liverpool. Derby and Preston, the only teams that still had a mathematical chance of lift-ing the title, shared four goals in a cracker at the Baseball Ground. The Villa, having scored more goals than any other team, were still on top of the table which looked like this:

			home				away						
	pld	w	d	l	f	a	w	d	l	f	a	g.av	pts
1 Aston Villa	27	8	3	2	28	16	10	2	2	36	22	1.68	41
2 Sheff U	28	6	4	5	22	16	6	6	1	18	11	1.48	34
3 Derby	25	10	2	2	45	21	4	2	5	18	20	1.54	32
4 Liverpool	28	7	4	2	23	8	5	3	7	21	28	1.22	31
5 Preston	24	7	3	1	31	17	3	6	4	20	19	1.42	29
6 Bolton	26	6	3	3	19	13	5	3	6	18	21	1.09	28
7 Sheff W	26	7	4	2	24	11	1	6	6	10	22	1.03	26
8 Everton	25	6	1	5	30	22	5	2	6	18	24	1.04	25
9 N Forest	27	8	2	3	29	14	1	5	8	14	30	0.98	25
10 Bury	25	6	4	3	23	14	2	5	5	12	23	0.95	25
11 Blackburn	28	8	1	6	27	25	3	2	8	8	33	0.60	25
12 W Brom	26	6	2	6	15	16	3	3	6	12	29	0.60	23
13 Wolves	26	5	4	5	22	14	3	2	7	15	20	1.09	22
14 Sunderland	28	4	6	5	21	21	2	2	9	11	25	0.70	20
15 Stoke	26	5	3	3	24	17	3	0	12	18	41	0.72	19
16 Burnley	27	3	5	5	18	22	2	2	10	18	33	0.65	17

On Monday 29th March, three Villa players helped England to a 4-0 victory over Wales. The Villa men would have enjoyed that victory more than anyone else in the team because in goal for the Welsh was none other than James Trainer. Still, none of the Lions could beat him although Athersmith had a goal ruled out for offside.

Joining Charlie on International duty were Howard Spencer, who had a quiet afternoon but did everything he had to perfectly, and Baldy Reynolds who was simply outstanding as a late replacement for Crabtree. Athersmith himself set up Bloomer for England's second on 43 minutes. The Derby man partnered Charlie on the right but didn't service him anything like as well as Devey did at the Villa. Even so, whenever 'Speedy' got the ball he crucified the unfortunate Welsh backs. No surprise there!

The absence of Crabtree from the England line-up threw further doubt on his ability to make the Cup Final. There were still twelve days to go to the big one and hopes were high that Jimmy would be passed fit and so allow Villa to chose from their strongest squad.

All Villa had to do now was prepare for the match at Crystal Palace, while Everton had one more League game before they could turn their attentions to the Final. FA Cup fever had gripped both Liverpool and Birmingham. On 10th April 1897, the supporters of those cities' greatest football clubs would descend on London and completely take over the Capital. What a day that turned out to be!

Chapter Ten

The Right Partnership
John Devey and Charlie Athersmith

It should now be apparent that Aston Villa had an incredibly strong squad in 1896/7. Apart from times of terrible injury crises - say four or five regulars being unable to play - they could field genuinely great players in the nine positions we have looked at. So that just leaves two spots to fill and, it must be said, in the inside and outside right berths Villa could not claim to have 'greats'.

Instead, the Club was blessed with a right-wing pair who, both individually and especially in combination, exceeded mere greatness by miles. John Devey (captain, great leader, expert dribbler, most tactically aware member of an entire team of fine tacticians) and Charlie Athersmith (possessor of blistering speed, silky skills and astonishing crossing ability) were, quite simply, from another planet. Were there any justice in the football world, these two men would automatically be mentioned whenever the question is asked: 'Who's the greatest of all time?' To lay one's cards on the table, it was Charlie Athersmith - just - and the evidence to back up such a seemingly rash statement will arrive shortly.

First, though, the skipper. And what a skipper he was! The only man to captain two Villa Cup winning teams, he also led his men to five League titles all in the space of eight years. That would be enough to guarantee anyone 'superstar' status, but Devey went on to serve his club in so many ways during an unbroken 43 year association, that he deserves elevation to the rank of Villa deity.

His story begins in the Newtown area of Birmingham where, on Boxing Day 1866, the infant John was born. His formative years were spent in Lozells, close enough to Heathfield Road to have been walking down THE street at the exact moment Aston Villa sprang to life! Even if he didn't pass within earshot of the gaslight group, growing up where he did he could only have been a fan of the Claret and Blues and couldn't help but be drawn under the spell of that unique Villa aura.

The best of Villa's brilliant bunch of all-round sportsmen, it was football that was Devey's first love. As a youth he had a prodigious talent which the amateur Birmingham Excelsior club spotted, and for whom he lined up at centre forward at the tender age of 16. During the two years he was at

Excelsior he played many home matches at the Aston Lower Grounds. Of course, this became Villa Park and John Devey - though he wouldn't know it in his amateur days - was destined to be the first player in a first-class match to take to the hallowed turf of that famous stadium.

John Devey

Devey turned professional at 18 when he moved to Aston Unity. By this time he was considered the second best forward in the Midlands, the best being none other than the legendary Villa captain, Archie Hunter. With such a reputation, it was assumed that the Villa would move in for Devey, but the call didn't come. Instead, in 1887, Mitchell's St. George's took on young John. At that time, Mitchell's were vying with Small Heath for the title of second best team in Brum and the purchase of such a gifted forward helped give them the edge. Yet still it was expected that he would come to Perry Barr, with the press regularly stating that a deal was being sorted out. Then, in 1888, Villa did sign Devey - but it wasn't John. Instead, it was his Uncle Harry who joined from Excelsior where, a couple of years earlier, he had lined-up as a half-back behind his nephew.

By the summer of 1890, Archie Hunter's failing health had finally put an end to his glittering career and the obvious replacement was still at Mitchell's. Devey did manage to turn out for Villa, in fact he captained the side - at Baseball! A brilliant exponent of America's national sport, John led the Club to trophy success. So good were Aston Villa at the game that they were often invited to give opposition to touring US sides, Devey's boys being one of the few outfits that could match the foreigners.

When the 1890/1 season began, Devey went back to his football employers and also opened a sports shop at Six Ways, Aston. It seemed that he would never play for his favourite club, but the speculation continued and, in February 1891, the press were able to confirm that he had signed for Aston Villa.

Amazingly, after all the calls to sign him up, many fans complained that the move had come too late and their new signing was too old. He was only 24, but because he had spent nearly a decade playing at a good level, everyone assumed him to be older. Thankfully the Villa Committee realised that he was the man for them and John made his full debut in the opening game of the 1891/2 campaign, scoring twice from the centre forward position in a 5-1 win over Blackburn.

During that season he missed only one match and joining him in thirteen games was his Uncle Harry. At the same time, John had two brothers playing together over at Small Heath. Some family! In all but three of his 1891/2 appearances, John played down the middle, the others being at inside right (twice) and one game at inside-left, thus he showed the trademark Villa versatility. But that otherwise happy campaign was marred by defeat in the Cup Final.

When George Ramsay signed John Devey, the *Birmingham Daily Post* commented: *"He is a great capture who will improve the forwards which have been so erratic of late. He is the best local centre forward since Archie Hunter was in his prime and although the Villa should have had him a couple of seasons ago, there is a lot of sterling stuff in Devey yet."*

Were they right? The England selectors thought so as they picked him for the game against Ireland in 1892. As for the scribe who wrote the above, he was a master of understatement. Devey's first campaign saw him easily top Villa's scoring charts with 29 from 25 League matches and 5 in 5 in the Cup. Yet that paled into insignificance in comparison with what was to come. At last plying his trade at Aston Villa, John Devey would enjoy a career the equal of which has arguably never been seen in any era.

The following season he again slotted into all three central forward positions, playing much of the season at inside left as Villa tried a number of players down the middle. Again Devey (who was ever-present) top-scored as the team secured fourth place in the League. They did, however, fall at the first hurdle in the Cup thanks to an incredible 5-4 reverse at Darwen in which Devey, somewhat predictably, found the net.

Having had two full seasons with the Club, Devey was about to become a central figure in an amazing run of success which saw Villa dominate football . 1893/4, as we already know, saw the Club lift the Championship for the first time. The undoubted player of that year was Devey who, for the third season running, headed Villa's goal-scoring chart. This time, he returned to the number '9' berth for most matches, from where he led his team to victory in his debut year as captain.

Once again, the England selectors recognised Devey's brilliance and picked him to line-up against Ireland. Yet, incredibly, he was never to win International honours again. The reason was that the selectors preferred Steve Bloomer of Derby and Preston's John Goodall. It is certainly difficult to justify a claim that any one of the three was discernably better than the others, but what was beyond all doubt - especially when Devey moved to inside right at the Villa - was that Devey brought the best out of Charlie Athersmith, England's regular right-winger. Reports from International matches of the day constantly refer to the lack of service Athersmith received, although they always mention how deadly he was once he had the ball. In this respect, the obvious answer was to pick Villa's skipper.

This lack of recognition was Devey's one big regret in an otherwise glittering career. He particularly wanted to play against Scotland. The fact that he didn't caused much joy in Glasgow where the Scottish selectors made no secret of the fact that they rated Devey as the best forward in the world. His dream unfulfilled, however, he had to make do with three appearances for the League against the Scottish League, the first coming in 1894. To round off a memorable season Devey made his county cricket debut that summer for Warwickshire, on whose books he had been since 1889.

He again faced the Tartan select in 1894/5, the season when revenge was gained over West Brom in the Cup Final. This, of course, was the game in which Devey scored the winner within half a minute of the start only to find his moment of glory credited to Bob Chatt. But, as should come as no surprise, the man who had been dismissed as 'past it' when he joined the Villa was highest scorer yet again. While the Committee still preferred to play Devey down the middle, he was getting more and more outings at inside-right where his partnership with Athersmith was showing signs of the awesome force it would become.

The opportunity for that right-wing marriage to really blossom came at the start of the '95/6 campaign when John Campbell joined the Villa. With Dennis Hodgetts at inside-left, Campbell was handed the number '9' shirt and the skipper linked up with 'Lightning' Charlie. Their combination was truly exceptional and opposing left-backs and halves finished matches against Aston Villa completely shell-shocked and bemused by the tantalising brilliance of the Devey - Athersmith pairing. These two linked up together amazingly well and fed Campbell with chance after chance as the Scotsman prevented Devey from being top scorer five years out of five. No doubt the team would have fared even better in front of goal but for injury to Hodgetts which saw Campbell and Devey shift over one place to the left as cover. Still, the League title was won meaning that in his first three seasons as captain, Devey had picked up the Cup once and the Championship twice.

We are currently reminiscing about the season in which Devey topped his previous achievements, so only a brief mention about '96/7 is required here. Having played his third and final game against the Scottish League at the end of the season, Devey was loaned out by Warwickshire to play for the famous Aston Unity Cricket Club in the Birmingham League. Unity - who played home games in Trinity Road - benefited greatly from the presence of this free-scoring opening batsman. For those familiar with this level of cricket, it would be fair to make comparison between Devey at Unity in 1897 and Asif Din at West Bromwich Dartmouth in 1996.

Having led his side to the Double, both Villa and Devey had a low-key 1897/8 season. As the Club got to grips with both key departures and injury problems, Devey saw nearly half the campaign ruled out as he joined Villa's list of walking wounded. But he came back with a bang the following year as he picked up his fourth League title and finished top-scorer.

At the same time, he hit the heights for Warwickshire, scoring his maiden and second first-class centuries against Hampshire (154) and Yorkshire (102). It was a similar story in season 1899/1900. Devey saw in the new century with another League Championship success and a massive score of 246 against Derbyshire. This still stands as the record score by a Warwickshire batsman against their East Midlands rivals.

Against such achievements, 1900/01 was a major come down. Villa slipped to their lowest ever placing of 15th in Division One and, even though Devey again proved the Club's most prolific hitman, his final season as captain saw further disappointment in the shape of a Cup semi-final replay defeat at the hands of Sheffield United.

Despite that sad end, Devey's eight years as skipper stand to this day as a memorial to the greatness of both Club and player. He was an ideal choice as captain as he was a thinking footballer, a fact which somewhat immodestly was not lost on Devey himself as this quote from the man shows:

"The captain should be the mouthpiece of the team; should be proud of his men; and his men should be proud of their captain. It is not necessary that the captain should be chosen merely because he is a hard worker... It is important that (he) should be able to set an example to his men in this respect, but... a man may be a great captain and yet lack the power to rank as the greatest worker. You play a captain for the manifestation of his brain power... You want the office of captain to be invested with a certain sense of dignity. The captain should be the brainiest man in the eleven; he should be looked up to by both management and players alike."

It wasn't all fun and games for Devey, however, as he led Aston Villa through their greatest period. Whilst the first half of his tenure was, unsurprisingly, filled with happiness, he had his difficult moments later on:

"The last four years of my captaincy at Aston Villa was the most trying period of my life. There comes a time when you cannot yourself do quite so much as you were once able to accomplish, and that is the time that the yearning for your old maximum power comes to you. You want a little help yourself then, and you do not always get it. That is a trying time indeed for a captain."

Devey was making reference to the 'star' players who showed little interest for minor matches and liked to play to the gallery. Those show-off types who felt certain jobs below them were detested by him. He also disliked the idea of having several skippers on the field, a position which seems diametrically opposed to the views of today when it is common to hear players and managers often eulogistically referring to the benefit of having eleven leaders in the team. John felt such a situation led to a *"conflict of authority."* But despite that hint at an 'iron hand' approach to his duties, Devey was a great believer in seeking the opinions of his players and would never stoop to dictatorial tactics.

And it was in the sphere of tactics that John Devey was truly the master of the captain's art. When talking of the 'Golden Days', Albert Evans would constantly refer with awe-struck deference to Devey's incredible ability to read the game and quickly counter any move that the opposition tried to make. Again, Devey's own words highlight this better than any second-hand account could:

"I can recall many occasions in the seasons when Aston Villa won the League Championship when diplomacy won us games in which our opponents were excessively dangerous. We would be occupied in resisting impetuous attacks when suddenly one of our men would get off; in would come a flying centre, the ball would come to John Campbell, he would send in one of his brilliant shots, and the whole position would be changed. We seldom received the credit for this to which we were entitled; it was not realised that we were following a carefully thought-out plan of campaign; sometimes we were told that we had scored a "lucky goal". There is more method in some of those lucky goals than some of the critics realise. You may have all watched games in which one side has manifested infinitely more devil for a given period than they have shown in any other portion of the match. It is the captain's duty to watch the play of his opponents during that period, and if he can cope with it he will have broken the backbone of that team."

So for eight years John Devey had done rather more that toss a coin every game. But, at the moment his captaincy concluded, so his career came to a fairly abrupt end. In the 1901/2 season he played in just four matches and, on 6th April 1902, he pulled on a claret and blue shirt for the last time, in a Birmingham and District League match.

Three months on from that sad, though inevitable, day, John Devey was elected to the Board of Directors. From there, that great leader helped guide the Club to further glories as they continued to amass silverware right up to the outbreak of World War 1. The captain's armband passed on to Howard Spencer who would, as we already know, join Devey on the Board when his own playing career ended.

While Devey could no longer keep up with the youngsters on the football pitch, his cricketing exploits continued down at Edgbaston. He finally ended an 18 year association with the County in 1907, twelve months after his benefit season which netted him £400. In his career, he played 324 innings scoring 7,659 runs at an average of 25.61. In the process, he posted eight centuries and was not out 20 times. To complete Devey's statistics, his occasional bowling appearances left a record of: 233.5 overs, 53 maidens, 655 runs, 16 wickets, average 40.93.

Devey continued his association with sport in Birmingham by taking various administrative posts. At Villa, he remained a director until September 1934. After that, he took his seat with the fans and rarely missed a Villa game. Devey had come full circle from the days when the Lozells-lad would hero-worship Archie Hunter.

John Devey saw Aston Villa share two goals with West Bromwich Albion at Villa Park on 19th August 1939. It turned out to be the last game he ever watched. On 11th October 1940, he died in a Birmingham nursing home. It is debatable if that great city has ever produced a better sportsman than Devey. He never left his home town, yet his name was mentioned with awe by rich and poor alike in every corner of the world. He may have been a Brummagem boy but, like the football club he became such an integral part of, his appeal and superstar status spread throughout the globe.

* * *

There are some who claim that John Devey would never have been the player he was without the presence of Charlie Athersmith alongside him. Others claim that Devey made Athersmith. Whatever the truth of either of these points of view, it is beyond doubt that there has never been a more brilliant pairing in any team, in any epoch, than Villa's wonderful right-wing of the 1890's.

Every era has produced players able to turn a game with a flash of inspiration. Aston Villa's Double winning team could, in addition to Devey and Athersmith, turn to Campbell, Wheldon, Smith, John Cowan, Reynolds or Crabtree to produce the unexpected. But where the right-side duo differed was that, as well as being supremely talented individuals, they possessed the kind of understanding which made them near on unstoppable. The sight of just one of the two racing goalwards was enough to scare the life out of the opposition. The pair of them bearing down in combination was the stuff of defenders' nightmares.

Both had extraordinary skills which could unlock the tightest rearguards, but they also possessed a great awareness of the other's whereabouts which allowed them to zip passes between themselves as they terrorised left-backs and halves. One touch football was their speciality and they were easily the best exponents of it.

The skipper's life has been detailed and it is now Charlie's turn. Not quite as local as Devey, Athersmith was born in Bloxwich in 1872. Very early on he was marked out as a gifted sportsman. For a start, he was far and away the fastest runner in his district. Allied to this was an ability to perform amazing tricks with a football, and control the sphere whilst losing none of his pace.

With such an abundance of talent, he found himself lining up for Bloxwich Wanderers at the tender age of eleven. He was, of course, not playing against adults - or at least not very often! But he frequently had to dodge the attentions of older, bigger and less sophisticated defenders who, despite their attempts to kick the frail boy off the park, could not get close to young Charlie. This set a pattern, for throughout his career it was rare that anyone got in a legitimate challenge on arguably the greatest player of all time.

Charlie Athersmith

Away from the football field, he also became a star of the athletics track. In his own age group, and quite a few above, he was easily the best quarter miler in the Midlands as well as being close to unbeatable at other sprint distances. His early years consisted of sport, sport and more sport as he found himself constantly changing between football boots and running shoes and back again.

Before he turned fifteen, Charlie was snapped up by Saltley's Unity Gas junior team, who were particularly successful at the six-a-side game. Athersmith's silky skills were shown off to great effect in this version of the sport in which he won numerous honours. People would come from far and wide to see the gifted teenager and his fame spread throughout the Midlands in a way that most seasoned professionals could only dream of.

Unsurprisingly, George Ramsay kept a close eye on the development of the starlet, waiting for the right moment to pluck him from his junior foot-balling education and bring him to the Villa. In December 1890, reports of Athersmith's signing began to appear, but he first turned up for training at Perry Barr in January 1891. There was concern at the time that, in the light of his blossoming career in athletics, he would wish to cling on to his amateur status. This proved to be unfounded, however, as Charlie immediately embraced professionalism and signed a League form for Aston

Villa. It turned out to be a union made in heaven.

One of the earliest games Charlie played for his new club was against Small Heath at Perry Barr. Although it was billed as a 'friendly', it turned out to be anything but. McKnight of the Villa became involved in a full-blooded fight with Small Heath's Jenkins. That might not have been so bad but for the fact that the latter was an ex-policeman! As for Athersmith, the *Birmingham Weekly Post* claimed he looked very good but: *"...lacks finish and will want a considerable amount of polish to make him first-class."*

He must have been buffed up a treat by some-one at the Villa for it would be an understatement to call him 'first-class'. He made his full debut in a 1-0 home defeat by Preston North End on 9th March 1891. Five days later he gave the world awesome notice of intent by netting a hat-trick as Wolves left Perry Barr having been handed a 6-2 thrashing.

Season 1891/2 saw Athersmith miss just two matches and pick up a Cup runners-up medal. The team were somewhat inconsistent but their young outside-right was superb in every game as Villa's forwards showed up brilliantly throughout. Charlie celebrated his first full League campaign by win-ning his first International cap. He joined John Devey in the England team to face the Irish. He wouldn't wear the Three Lions again for five years. The following year again saw him in blistering form and although he was among the less versatile of the Villa squad, he still filled in at both inside-right and centre forward during 1892/3. Later in his career, he would also line-up in the inside-left berth.

The 1894 Championship campaign saw Athersmith really come good. Consequently, the England selectors were heavily criticised for over-looking the flying winger. For the third season run-ning he reached double-figures in goals scored while his crossing had become so good that it was almost unheard of that a Charlie centre didn't find a Villa man. Much of the right-wing responsibility fell solely on his shoulders as Villa failed to play a regular inside-right, but Charlie showed great maturity to carry his burden with incredible style. His reward came with the first of seven League representative honours against the Scottish League.

He again took on the Scots XI in '94/5, his first ever-present season for the Villa. It was in the thrilling opening to that year's Cup Final that Athersmith's speed was shown at its destructive best. From the kick-off, he simply galloped down the right with the ball held magnetically to his mag-ical feet. He beat two challenges, reached the goal-line and centred. Bob Chatt caught the ball on the half volley, Reader saved with his feet and the ball hit Devey's knee and rebounded into the net. The goal - which was dubbed the 'Crystal Palace Thunderbolt' - may have been the subject of historical inaccuracy, but what is beyond doubt is that it was Charlie's brilliance which won the Cup for Villa.

A year later, Athersmith picked up his second Championship medal having missed just one match in the campaign. Interestingly enough, that absence coincided with Aston Villa suffering their only dropped point at home all season. Although he only scored eight goals - a figure more than made up for by the amount he laid on - his best game came in the 5-1 home win against Burnley in which he scored his second and final hat-trick for the Club.

Before the amazing 1896/7 season got under way, there was intense speculation that Athersmith was on his way out of Perry Barr. It was reported that he had written to the Villa Committee to say that he was joining Everton on a three year contract. It was further alleged that a disagreement over his entitlement to a benefit match had caused Charlie's disenchantment with the Club. In another example of how in depth press reports - even ones based on fabricated evidence - were at the time, the papers said Everton would be paying the winger £5.10s per week all year round.

The last point should have given a clue that the alleged letter from Athersmith was a forgery, for he was then Villa's highest paid player on a year round weekly wage of £6.10s. It was true that Club and player were negotiating details regarding a possible benefit, but Charlie never had any intention nor desire to leave Aston Villa. He did, however, admit that Everton were interested in him, and reportedly claimed that every club would be glad of his services. However, no other side ever made an official approach to Villa, probably because they knew he was priceless!

It was fortunate for both Charlie and his employers that he didn't seek employment elsewhere, for if '96/7 was Villa's greatest moment, to Athersmith it represented the pinnacle of his career. By April, he had claimed a place in history with a feat no other player before or since can match. Having collected League and Cup winners medals, he went on to gain his caps against Ireland, Wales and Scotland and faced the Scottish League. This meant that Charlie Athersmith won every available honour in a single season. It is true that there are more honours available nowadays, making it nigh on impossible to match this record. But it should be remembered that International caps were not handed out as cheaply as in modern times and even Preston's great 1889 'Invincibles' failed to produce a player to match Charlie's achievements.

If 1897/8 was a moderate campaign by Villa's standards, the only difference for Athersmith was that he failed to repeat his achievement of being ever-present as he was in the Double year. Once again he played in all three Internationals and against the Scottish League. The latter - a 2-1 defeat - took place at Villa Park before 22,000 spectators. Charlie also received his benefit on Monday 13th September 1897 in a match of mixed emotions against Derby County. In a 6-2 win, the man himself scored twice but was outgunned by hat-trick hero, Fred Wheldon. Sadly, though, Jimmy Whitehouse was injured in the game and it took him three months to regain fitness!

Two days previous, Athersmith produced one of his regular matchwinning displays in a League match at Notts. County. In the 88th minute of the game, Villa were trailing 2-1 and looking a beaten combination. County were dominating and there seemed no way out for the Lions. The ball was scrambled out to Charlie who was back inside his own half. He reached the ball just ahead of his marker and proceeded to race down the wing. Looking up he spotted John Cowan coming in at the far post and whipped in a deadly accurate centre which saw Cowan bring Villa back on level terms.

At that point, the visiting fans would have settled gladly for a point, but they and County reckoned without the genius lurking menacingly on the right-wing. As the clock ticked down like a scene from a James Bond film, Athersmith again received the ball around halfway. This time, it was from a measured pass by John Devey. The skipper continued his forward run while his wing partner evaded no less than four challenges as he carried the ball deep into enemy territory. Having neared the corner flag, he looked as if he would be boxed in, but found space to deliver another pinpoint centre for Devey to slam home the winner. Notts. barely had time to kick-off before the game was called to a close.

It was the kind of scenario more readily associated with *Roy of the Rovers.* For Charlie, whilst such a spectacular show wasn't a common occurrence, it was not the first, nor the last, time he would single-handedly win a game for his side. The game at Trent Bridge represented further evidence to back the claim that he was one of the greatest players ever to lace up a pair of boots. Few men, if any, throughout footballing history can claim to have the talent to affect games the way Athersmith could and did.

Back to Championship winning ways in 1898/9, Athersmith picked up his trio of caps for the third year running and again won a place in the League

XI. But the undoubted highlight was the International against Scotland. In the most prestigious football match in the world, he joined Jimmy Crabtree in the England team as 22,000 people witnessed the first ever Full International to be held at Villa Park. For the record, the Villa men played on the winning side, snatching victory by the odd goal in three.

As the new Century was rung in with another Villa title, Athersmith suffered his longest ever spell out of the team as injury kept him absent for seven consecutive matches. The 1899/1900 season also saw him win the last of his caps as he wore the White Shirt against both Wales and Scotland. As was now almost expected, he again terrorised the left-hand side of the Scottish League Select.

The following season was a real turning point for the Club as the Committee sought to rebuild. That partly explains Villa's abysmal campaign, although Athersmith was the one bright spark in a best forgotten eight months. The main problem for the team was that no one seemed able to find the net. Billy Garraty was forced to spend much of his time in the unfamiliar inside-left position as no regular 'natural' number 10 could be fielded. Charlie was still doing the business on the wing, but his brilliant approach play was not capitalised on by the rest of the team.

His final matches of the season, and of his Villa career, were hugely disappointing even though his performance on the ball was as had come to be be expected. His last League outing for the Club saw him at inside-left in a 3-0 reversal at Newcastle. In the Cup, it was at inside-right that Charlie bade his Villa farewell in the semi-final replay against Sheffield United at the Baseball Ground, when again Villa conceded three without reply.

There was some consolation for Athersmith as he faced the Scottish League for the fifth season running. But, in June 1901, he moved to Small Heath for whom he would top 100 appearances. The reason for his short trip across Birmingham was simply that Ramsay, Rinder and Grierson were looking to the future and obviously felt that Charlie was living on borrowed time and would prevent young fresh talent from emerging. The theory cannot be faulted but in practice it is impossible to better a player of the ability of Athersmith. Villa's loss was the Blues' gain.

Before rounding off Charlie's career, it is worth reflecting on his talent in an attempt to justify the earlier contention that he was the greatest footballer of all time. At this point, it may be appropriate to note the style of press reporting in those days. Match reports were a hybrid of the modern day examples carried by the Sports Argus and the Birmingham Evening Mail: that is to say they contained kick-by-kick coverage of entire sections of play interspersed with comment and analysis.

Very often, one would read of numerous attacks which broke down, but - having read hundreds of reports - the author has yet to come across a single example of a journalist stating that Athersmith lost the ball or misplaced a pass. There were plenty of occasions when he would shoot 'just wide' or force the 'keeper into a save, but it seems he was never tackled nor did he give possession away through poor play.

It is, of course, highly unlikely that this was the case, but the lack of critical reporting suggests that Athersmith being robbed of the ball or failing to find a team-mate was exceedingly, extraordinarily, rare.

His speed was legendary. When all other tactics failed, or the rest of the team were out of sorts, a pass to Athersmith would see the winger simply outstrip his opponents for pace. If he was faced with a clever back who would attempt to 'jockey' him and close Charlie down, he would beat his opponent with skill. And this is the key to his genius. He could maintain his blistering speed with the ball at his feet and under perfect control.

He was two-footed, his armoury of tricks could not be improved upon. His distribution was first-class in that he could send balls any required distance with perfect accuracy. His shooting was also usually accurate although he was not a prolific scorer by any means. That said, there were often men better placed to score than Charlie and he would always pick them out.

Most of all, he really could transform a game and claim a win through his own individual efforts. If it is unreasonable to place Athersmith above the likes of Pele, Eusebio, Matthews and Gullit, it would be equally wrong to ignore Charlie - as is, without fail, done - when waxing lyrical about the merits of these post-war greats.

There were only two ways to stop Charlie. The first was to attempt to kick him off the park. This was tried by most defenders in most matches. To begin with they had to get near him. That done, they had to get their violence in while he was still within striking distance. If this happened too many times, Charlie would soon dish out his (often highly crude) retaliation. Even 'thug' tactics, though, failed to diminish the threat the winger posed.

The second method of keeping him quiet was to starve him of service. This was impossible in Villa games because of the telepathic nature of his partnership with John Devey. In International matches, however, he would often go for long periods without seeing the ball. But when he did get it, one could be guaranteed that he would torment the opposition mercilessly.

The press of the 1890's was a highly critical one. Further, unlike so many of today's journalists who seem to reserve praise for a select few whilst certain other personalities are forced to suffer an avalanche of brickbats, the Victorian scribes did not possess favourites who were beyond criticism. Rather, they told it as they saw it. Everyone faced criticism at some time or another, except Charlie Athersmith. The reason for this was that he never deserved to be criticised. Certain supporters sometimes had bad comments to make about him, but they were rarely justified.

Returning to Athersmith's final days in football, after he left Small Heath his life was - to quote from his obituary in the *Birmingham Daily Post* - "...*rather a chequered one.*" The article continues: "*He had a good bank balance when he played at Aston, but we fear (says the "Athletic News") that he did not increase that balance as the result of what happened when he took a licensed house at Bloxwich.*"

He was forced to give up his pub and took the job of team trainer at Grimsby Town in 1907. Two years later, he came back to the Midlands and returned to the licensed trade by buying a bar in Redditch. This too failed.

Despite the fact that he had been a very healthy man and once commented that: "*I have had no serious illness since I was a boy of fourteen*", Athersmith died suddenly at his mother's house in Oakengates, Shropshire on Sunday 18th September 1910, leaving a widow and one child. It was widely rumoured that his death resulted from a kick in the stomach which he received during his playing days. The injury caused more damage than was thought and resurfaced years later to do for poor Charlie.

The *Birmingham Gazette and Express* carried a tribute to Athersmith by "Old Fogey" and which is worthy of reproduction here:

"*What a player he was, and how people used to enjoy those daring and dazzling runs of his! ... They used to call him 'Spry' - and he was that! He was more sinned against than sinning. Why, the very clumsiness of his reprisals proved that he was not a 'dirty' player. Let me tell you why. Charlie was about the fastest Association player performing in the heyday of his fame, and not only his comrades but his opponents knew it. Both used to take steps accordingly ("taking steps" is just right in this connection) - one to help him along; the other to stop his gallop if possible - and he couldn't half gallop! It (was) great fun to see Jack Devey tempt defenders to himself and then suddenly* shoot the ball to Athersmith, who would mill serenely and succinctly along the line (for he could dribble purely at a rush) and whiz it across for the other chaps to clear up a good job well begun; and they very often did it. I should say that the tactics I have thus hurriedly and roughly described gained the Villa more goals than any other series of movements; and I remember how James Cowan (prince and paragon of centre half-backs) had the happy knack of speeding the leather to the accomplished Athersmith.*

"*There was another side to the picture, however, and it was not such a pleasant one. Opponents of the baser sort made up their minds to stop him - by fair means, if they could (which they generally couldn't); but to stop him anyhow. And I have seen him tripped and hacked and bashed mercilessly till the referee interfered, till the right-winger's blood got on the boil, and then he'd occasionally turn and take reprisals in quite a flagrantly open way; many folk blaming him who had not noticed the aforesaid tricks to stop him. When Athersmith was at his best there was no man playing who received more 'attention' of one sort or another; and yet he never received 'marching orders' during the whole of his splendid career.*

"*Charlie Athersmith had a long and very brilliant career, and for a man of his football attainments he was wonderfully consistent. Fact is, he thoroughly and honestly enjoyed the game, and from first to last played it for all he was worth.*"

Charlie, like most geniuses, was always a little on the wild side. He was never quite tamed. This should not be misunderstood, however. He was never as bad as some gifted footballers one could mention. But he had this air of freedom about him which perfectly suited the free-flowing expressive Aston Villa of the 1890's. The combination of player and Club was too hot to handle for the rest of the game's finest.

No biography - however potted - of Charlie Athersmith would be complete without mention of the most famous and oft told tale about the great man. It is said that on a particularly wet day, Athersmith played a match whilst holding an umbrella to protect himself from the elements. Now, the author cannot claim to have undertaken exhaustive research, but as yet no contemporary report of the 'umbrella' incident has surfaced. It is not known whether Charlie brought the rain-guard out with him, if a supporter handed it to him, for how long he played 'under cover' nor, indeed, whether or not the incident took place. However, it is so much a part of Villa folklore that the details no longer matter.

What can be said with absolute certainty is that such an incident would perfectly fit Charlie's personality. There was a cheeky humour about the man and, anyway, he could have crucified any defence whilst wearing a three-piece suit, bowler hat and carrying a briefcase to match his umbrella. Yes, such a tale could only be linked to the inimitable Charlie Athersmith.

* * *

The Athersmith - Devey partnership was famed and feared throughout the world and continued to receive its due credit right up to the Second World War. Then, inexplicably, it was forgotten by football pundits and fans alike. It is a pity that television was not around to capture this great duo at work. If it had been, apart from giving us all the opportunity to see their astounding ability, it would have meant that modern-day commentators would understand that football is not just about players who have been visually recorded for posterity. The game and some of its greatest exponents were around way back into the last Century and the memory of both should be kept alive.

Chapter Eleven

The Double

In Birmingham, there was talk of nothing else. The Double was there for the taking. The fans swamped the Club with requests for saloon carriages to take them to the Cup Final. George Ramsay had the unenviable task of wading through the mountain of ticket applications whilst William McGregor haggled with the railway companies in an attempt to get the best deals for Aston Villa's faithful followers.

Joe Grierson and James Lees took the players off to Buxton Hydro for five days immediately after the win at Bolton, boosted by the news from Manchester that James Crabtree should be fit for the big match. It was good to have two clear weeks to prepare for the showdown with Everton, but the management duo had to make sure that the players weren't given too long to dwell on the importance of their forthcoming task.

Saturday 3rd April 1997 was a big day for many reasons. Three games took place which had relevance to the clubs competing for the world's most famous sports trophy. One of these matches saw the following squad travel to Bristol for a friendly match against Eastville Rovers:

Whitehouse, Bourne, Welford (temporarily back in the fold), Burton, Crawford, Johnstone, Smith, Harris, Campbell, Wheldon, Harvey and John Cowan.

The reason for so many unfamiliar names in that line-up was that it was decided to rest some of the stars. Also, Jas Cowan for Scotland and Charlie Athersmith and John Reynolds for England were in London for the International at Crystal Palace, giving them the opportunity to get acclimatised to the Cup Final arena. Meanwhile, in the League, Preston entertained Everton in a game which saw the home side run out 4-1 winners. The result met with a mixed response from the Villa. On the one hand it was hardly ideal preparation for the Liverpudlians, but it did mean that Preston still had a chance of lifting the title, no matter how unlikely such an outcome now seemed.

Back to the West Country. A year earlier, a Bristol and District League XI beat Villa. Billy George played in goal and, as we know, the club decided to take him home with them. The 1897 encounter did not unearth any claret and blue stars of the future, but a weak Villa eleven trotted out 5-0 winners.

Johnstone began a lovely move in the 15th minute which saw Smith and Cowan involved before Wheldon was released to open the scoring. About midway through the half, the hosts were reduced to ten men as Gallier retired having sustained a nasty gash to his right eye. But they defended resolutely and when the interval came, only a Smith strike had been added to the score sheet. Indeed, Rovers may have been better off sticking to ten men, for at half-time a sub was allowed for Gallier, but Villa scored straight from the resumption. Having launched a powerful attack from the kick-off which won a corner, Burton met the centre to head his side's third. Villa continued to press against a packed home defence. Smith got his second with a halfhearted shot and, whilst Eastville had a couple of good attacks, Harvey completed the rout five minutes from time.

At Crystal Palace, Scotland won the big battle 2-1. It was unanimously agreed that Jas Cowan was the star of a brilliant game. His halfback play was described as pure perfection. The only player on either side who came close to the heights of Jas was Baldy Reynolds who again showed the selectors why they were lucky to have such an exceptional replacement for Crabtree. It was Reynolds who began the move which led to England's strike. He found Athersmith who beat two backs before picking out the scorer, Steve Bloomer. For Charlie, though, it was another game where he was criminally under-used. He was the one England player who could really destroy the Scottish backs but didn't get the service from his team-mates. A call to John Devey would, of course, have remedied that problem.

* * *

By the evening of Sunday 4th April, both the Everton and Aston Villa squads were settled into their training camps at Lytham and Buxton Hydro respectively. Both sides prepared in secret. The Villa usually allowed the press free access to training camps. But this one was different and, whilst journalists were regularly updated with news of the squad, everything was done strictly behind closed doors.

James Crabtree returned from Manchester. He was vital for Villa's attempts to combat the Everton right-wing of Bell and Taylor and, of course, to support his own forwards. On Wednesday 7th April, Crabtree was given a most rigorous fitness test which included sprinting and plenty of ball work. He passed with flying colours thus meaning that Aston Villa could select from their strongest possible squad. That squad was narrowed down to the following who would travel to London:

Jimmy Whitehouse, Howard Spencer, Albert Evans, John Reynolds, Jas Cowan, Jimmy Crabtree, Charlie Athersmith, John Devey, John Campbell, Fred Wheldon, John Cowan, Tom Wilkes, Frank Burton and Steve Smith.

The release of the above list put paid to one piece of speculation. It was now known that James Welford would not replace young Albert Evans at left-back. The only question now was who would get the left-wing berth: Steve Smith or John Cowan.

Before Villa made the trip south, their attention was momentarily focused on the Town Ground, Nottingham where on Thursday 8th April Forest entertained Preston North End. The latter had to win to maintain any possibility of catching the League Champions. Not surprisingly with their keeper being in such fine form, North End did not concede a goal. Fortunately or not (depending upon who one supports) they didn't score either. One down and one to go as Derby were now the only team left who could prevent the Pets from retaining their title.

* * *

The following day the exodus began. The first train loads of supporters from Liverpool and Birmingham travelled south-east, their destination the Capital. These were the fans who were going to take the opportunity to spend the whole weekend in London, the Cup Final being just one part - albeit a somewhat large part - of what they hoped would be the holiday of a lifetime. The next twenty-four hours would not see a single under-subscribed train on the London-North West route.

The two sets of players and officials also journeyed south on the Friday. The Villa left Buxton at midday and headed straight for their headquarters in Upper Norwood, a ten-minute walk from the Crystal Palace enclosure. The players could only be described as being in perfect condition. There was also the little matter of bonuses to keep their minds focused on the job in hand, although little is probably the wrong word. The Villa team were on a promise of up to £34 a man if John Devey collect-

ed the Cup. Additionally, there were fine clothes, cigars, liquor and other gifts offered by Birmingham's tradesmen if victory was secured.

Everton's squad of fourteen arrived in London at almost exactly the same time as their adversaries. The directors and officials made their way to the Tavistock Hotel, but the destination of the playing staff remained a closely guarded secret. They were reported to have had a fine training camp at Lytham and there was no doubt that they were in peak condition. They were also, like the Villa, highly confident of victory. This positive attitude was mirrored by supporters of both teams as well as the people of Birmingham and Liverpool. Nowhere in either city was defeat contemplated. The accents may have been different but the message was the same: *"We're going to win the Cup"*

All the players had to do now was relax, get a good night's sleep and stay off the beer. The latter instruction would not have been needed in the Everton camp. Whilst Aston Villa had pretty much made the Old Crown and Cushion their headquarters for the previous 21 years, the Toffeemen led a far more Quakerish lifestyle with seven of their number being total abstainers!

* * *

There is no more special day. It always starts early for the followers of the Cup Final elevens. Seven o'clock and New Street Station fades into the background for the fans who have crammed themselves on to the first of the Cup Specials. Four more left in the following hour, whilst the official party organised by the Club departed at 9:15. In addition to the London and North West Railway Company's excursions, Cooks ran two trains and a number left from Redditch. But the one to be on was the GWR Special. At twenty past eight on Saturday 10th April 1897, a massive mechanical snake heaved out of Snow Hill Station. The claret and blue festooned carriages bulged with Villamen as the engine gathered up the speed which would carry them to a date with destiny at Crystal Palace. It was a similar story at Liverpool Lime Street where a sea of blue and white engulfed the platforms.

Elsewhere in Lancashire, supporters of tenth-placed Bury had rather less travelling to do. At Gigg Lane, their side were playing hosts to a Derby team currently occupying the runners-up spot. Villa fans were probably too engrossed in their own game to give this League match a second thought, but it would prove a vital element of the day that saw Aston Villa claim a unique place in football history.

* * *

There was a record number of them. 65,891 people packed the stands. At that time they represented the largest Cup Final crowd ever and possibly the biggest attendance at any football match played anywhere in the world. The stands appear to fill slowly as the mass shuffles laboriously through the turnstiles. But by three o'clock the ground is bursting at the seams for this battle of the Titans.

The Crystal Palace football pitch - which, like the Villa Park surface, was a filled-in lake - had been properly christened two years previously when Villa defeated Albion in the 1895 Cup Final. Everton exited the pavilion first to be greeted by an incredible roar which lasted fully two minutes. As the noisy Liverpudlians quietened down, the Brummie voices showed Crystal Palace that they too could belt out their support as the Villa hit the field.

In the Pavilion Stand, former Prime Minister Lord Rosebery and his two sons were joined by Lord Kinnaird, himself a five times Cup winner with the Wanderers. Along with the rest of the massive assemblage, they saw the following line-ups battle for the ultimate honour:

ASTON VILLA

Whitehouse

Spencer   Evans

Reynolds   Jas Cowan   Crabtree

Athersmith Devey Campbell Wheldon John Cowan

Milward   Chadwick   Hartley   Bell   Taylor

Stewart   Holt   Boyle

Storrier   Meecham

Menham

EVERTON

Spare a thought for Everton's Arridge, Robertson and Williams who, like Tom Wilkes, Frank Burton and Steve Smith, had to watch from the stands.

The match officials were J. Halcroft of Redcar and J. Scragg from Crewe who ran the lines for referee John Lewis of Blackburn. That is the same John Lewis who awarded Villa a controversial goal in the 2-1 defeat of Notts County in the second round. An omen?

John Devey won the toss and chose to defend the north-east goal with the declining sun in the Villa players' faces and a mild easterly blowing over their shoulders. As was common in Cup finals, the game began at a blistering pace. It had been thought prior to the match that Everton would attempt to set a fast tempo in an attempt to ruffle

the Villa backs. In the event, they didn't have to because the Villa galloped away from the off. The first real break in an incredible opening came near the five minute mark when Holt achieved the impossible - he robbed Athersmith of the ball! The thing is, to accomplish this feat he had hurled himself at Villa's winger and succeeded in winding himself. The good old magic sponge soon had him on his feet again, but the brief respite his pain had afforded was most welcome to all. As Holt tried to breathe, players and spectators alike enjoyed their first chance to take breath.

Upon the restart, Villa continued to press Everton back. Crabtree and Athersmith combined on the right with the latter centring to Wheldon. His route to goal was blocked but he teed up John Cowan who was foiled by an alert rush from Meecham. The Villa right-wing drew massive cheers from the crowd as Devey and Athersmith quickly got their brilliant passing game together. Three attacks in quick succession were instigated by these two men who were mesmerising the discomfited Blue backs. For fully five minutes, the ball remained in the Everton half.

When the Toffeemen did break out, they found Howard Spencer in supreme form. He half cleared a dangerous move and, to great howls of approval from the stands, Reynolds completed the job by heading the ball away whilst he was on all fours.

Brilliantly supported by their half-backs, the Villa forwards took a grip on the match. Wheldon, Campbell, Devey and Athersmith left the Everton backs chasing shadows as they combined to set up the first-named who shot narrowly over. The same four were again involved a minute later with a move that ended with Athersmith just skimming the crossbar. Hartley relieved the pressure slightly when he drew a foul from Jas Cowan. Both sets of players were fully committed and the challenges were as strong as one would expect with so much at stake.

The Villa continued to bombard their opponents. Twice John Campbell worked openings. His first effort flew wide but his second forced a fine fingertip save from Menham. But as the Claret and Blues pressed, they left themselves open to a counter, if only Everton could get the ball. They got their chance on the quarter hour and suddenly Holt, Chadwick and Milward were bearing down on the solitary figure of Howard Spencer. With such odds, there could only be one winner... and sure enough the Prince of Full-Backs came away with the ball to set up another Villa attack.

On 18 minutes, John Devey received a pass from Baldy Reynolds and produced a piece of real magic. Athersmith peeled away into space and everyone assumed the ball would soon follow.

Devey moved to play Charlie in but, unbeknown to the Everton players, he had spotted a run by John Campbell. Devey hooked his foot round the ball and sent a perfectly weighted ball along the deck, straight through the heart of the opposition.

The on-rushing Campbell took the ball in his stride, glanced up and with frightening power and precision placement he crashed his shot past Menham and into the top corner of the net from 25 yards out. As goals go, it at least matches Savo Milosevic's opener in the League Cup Final of 1996 for the shot was very similar yet the build up far more polished. The *Birmingham Daily Post* reported: *"A roar of applause went up from the crowd who could not help admiring the clever play of the greatest team in the country."*

The next few minutes saw Villa - and especially their right-wing - cut through Everton at will. A foul on Wheldon resulted in a free-kick which was nudged to Reynolds. Baldy, the crowd's favourite, unleashed a ferocious effort which scraped the top of the crossbar.

Everton, though, regrouped marvellously. Villa were saved when Hartley was called narrowly offside. Five minutes after Villa had taken the lead, that player then produced a great pass which enabled John Bell to round Spencer. He raced clear on goal leaving Whitehouse no choice but to come out. Bell saw the 'keeper advancing and coolly placed the ball into the goal. As it hit the net, so Whitehouse and Bell hit each other. They both needed treatment before the game could restart.

The goal gave Everton a much needed shot in the arm, but still play raced from end-to-end. 28 minutes had elapsed when Jas Cowan gave away a foul in a dangerous position. Stewart sent a free-kick into the danger area and, following a slight melee, Boyle connected to send Everton in front and their supporters wild. Villa had been the better side yet found themselves 2-1 down.

Everton remained dangerous but the Villa began to regain the upper hand. Their persistence paid off in the 38th minute. John Cowan and Fred Wheldon used their sublime skills to work an opening down the left. Cowan laid the ball off to the supporting Crabtree who passed deftly to Wheldon. Fred shot hard and low leaving Menham with no chance. The score was level once more.

The pace of this ding-dong battle hadn't slowed one bit. Both leftbacks had to be at their best to thwart good attacks as the gladiators sought to edge in front. Young Albert Evans was putting in an astonishingly good performance which made a mockery of claims that he lacked the experience needed for such a big game.

His opposite number, Storrier, was being worn down by Athersmith and Devey. Again and again Charlie teased the poor back who was playing exceptionally well but learning the hard way that some players just can't be stopped. Storrier flung himself at the ball to save Everton with his head at the expense of a corner. Athersmith took it short to Reynolds who sent Storrier in circles as he played it back to Charlie who returned the ball to Baldy. The cross from Reynolds' trusty right boot found his opposite winghalf as Jimmy Crabtree capped his comeback by heading Villa in front two minutes from half-time. It was his first goal of the season.

Five goals had been scored in the space of 25 minutes and the crowd realised that they were watching perhaps the best game of football ever played. Both sides had good attacks in the remaining couple of minutes, but neither made their possession tell so Aston Villa ended an incredible half with an advantage of 3 to 2.

Attacking the Palace End goal and with the wind at their backs, Everton started the second half brightly. Evans kept a cool head to partially clear during a goal-mouth scramble, but the ball fell to Milward whose blistering shot was brilliantly turned away by Whitehouse. Then Villa broke away and won a free-kick following a hand ball incident. From that, Reynolds hit a fantastic shot which dipped late but just cleared the crossbar.

The second period, understandably, was not played at quite the pace of the first, but the teams remained evenly matched with the advantage swinging one way and then back again. Everton were showing no sign of fatigue despite claims that they lacked the fitness to last with the top teams. Both 'keepers had to produce top form to keep the score sheet static. Devey and Athersmith caused trouble at one end whilst John Bell produced the game of his life at the other, only to be denied by the greatest half-backs in the land. Both sides were producing such brilliant play that partisanship was all but forgotten by the crowd who marvelled at the spectacle unfolding before them. This truly was football at its best.

Everton began to get on top as they desperately looked for the strike that would level matters. Bell lost out in a one-on-one with Whitehouse, having worked himself into the same position from which he had scored his side's first. A Boyle free-kick scraped the bar and Evans tackled brilliantly to deny Taylor. But Villa were dangerous on the break. Athersmith (who else?) sped away down the right before cutting the ball inside for Jas Cowan. His first shot was blocked but he got a second bite only to see Menham turn his low, goal-bound effort wide. Then Campbell carried the ball down the middle from deep. A neat one-two with Devey left the centre-forward with a great chance but he slipped as he made contact, leaving a grateful Menham to collect easily.

The game continued to ebb back and forth. Everton found themselves goal-side of the backs but, before they could test Whitehouse, Reynolds recovered to hook the ball away. At the other end, Campbell brought his right-wing into play and a great ball from Devey gave Athersmith the chance to screw a cross into the danger area. Campbell met it in the air but his header missed the goal by no more than a few inches.

The pace suddenly picked up to the level of the first half. Attacks at one end were quickly followed by attacks at the other and even the crowd seemed relieved when a foul or a player's need for treatment produced a pause. But, unlike in the opening 45 minutes, this time the defences reigned supreme.

The last ten minutes saw Everton go all out for victory and their injection of pace initially took Villa by surprise. Twice Bell brought great saves out of Whitehouse before Chadwick hit a shot which would have beaten just about every 'keeper (Trainer apart perhaps) in the land. The Villa custodian launched his athletic frame and brilliantly turned the ball round his far post. It was the last time he was called into action as the Villa defence stifled their opponents. Villa were content to sit back and soak up everything Everton had to throw at them. They even managed the odd breakaway and, with every Villa fan believing their watches to have stopped, two minutes of keep-ball by the Villa forwards ended with a Campbell shot which left Menham to make the final save of the game. One reporter described the final quarter of an hour as: *"...a serious nerve trial to witness"* for any Villa fan. But their boys had done it and in the most marvellous manner. Everton belied their mid-table status and demonstrated that with a little consistency they might become Villa's equals. As John Lewis called matters to a halt, no one could doubt that Everton had played an heroic part in a great Cup Final.

At the end of the match the crowd surged on to the pitch and carried their heroes shoulder high to the Pavilion. Every spectator knew that they had witnessed the best Cup Final ever. The simple fact was that throughout the entire ninety minutes there wasn't a single dull moment. Only two Finals have since come close to recapturing the standard of the 1897 classic. Only the 'Stanley Matthews' Final of 1953 and the titanic struggle between Arsenal and Manchester United in 1979 were at all comparable with the exceptional encounter of Aston Villa and Everton.

For Villa, and for that matter Everton, all the players played magnificently. Athersmith and Devey were at their destructive best while John Campbell led the line well, found space for himself, shot menacingly and passed with accuracy throughout. On the left, Wheldon and John Cowan did everything expected on them but it is hard to shine when the bright lights of Villa's right-wing burn so fiercely. Fred and John were definitely the unsung heroes of the Final. The half-backs were outstanding. Crabtree lasted the pace well following his injury problems and Reynolds supported his forwards immaculately. As for Jas, the *Birmingham Daily Post* commented: *"He was the best player amongst twenty-two great ones."* Precisely as he was a week earlier in the International match. Spencer and Evans coped well with the excellent Everton forwards and showed amazing powers of improvisation in some hairy situations. And Whitehouse produced some great saves and was not at fault with the two shots that beat him. A glorious performance in a glorious match in a glorious setting to win a glorious competition.

But there was still the small matter of receiving the Cup. John Devey, that supreme leader of men, walked up the steps to be greeted by Lord Rosebery. Unlike today, there was no swift handshake and mumble of congratulations. The noble Lord instead delivered the following speech:

"It is my great honour and great privilege not only to have seen this splendid and Olympic contest, but to be chosen to present you with the cup which represents your hard earned victory. I suppose I have been chosen as being the greatest novice amongst the many thousands of spectators who enjoyed this exciting struggle. I cannot judge the finer points of the game, but I can judge the great qualities which both sides have displayed - those qualities which we distinctly recognise as British. For not merely have you shown every physical quality that men can show, but no one who has seen the game can deny that it requires great qualities of head as well."

This last comment drew chants of 'Reynolds' from the crowd. Lord Rosebery continued: *"I congratulate the winning eleven with all my heart and second and only second to them, I congratulate the Everton eleven for the magnificent fight they have made. Now gentlemen, some of us may be partisans of one side and some of the other, but there is one feeling which I can express I am certain on behalf of every spectator of the sixty or seventy thousand spectators that have seen this game. That is our thanks to you for having given us a splendid exhibition which no one who has seen will ever forget."*

He handed the trophy to John Devey who returned thanks on behalf of Aston Villa and proudly held aloft the Cup to the cheers of thousands of the supporters who had faithfully followed the team throughout this stunning season.

It took over an hour for the stadium to empty. The multitude made their way to trains which ferried the delighted and the dejected back to the centre of London. Everton returned to the Tavistock for what they had hoped would have been a celebration dinner. Instead, the party atmosphere was to be found just up the road where Upper Norwood played host to the party of the year. Well, it retained that title until the victors returned to Brum where the celebrations dwarfed anything one could imagine.

But there is one event from 10th April which still needs to be mentioned. When John Devey received the English Cup, no one at Crystal Palace had the slightest inkling of the little bit of history which had been made. Up at Bury, Derby had lost 1-0. The table below shows the significance of that result:

			home				away						
	pld	w	d	l	f	a	w	d	l	f	a	g.av	pts
1 Aston Villa	27	8	3	2	28	16	10	2	2	36	22	1.68	41
2 Derby	27	10	2	2	45	21	5	2	6	21	23	1.50	34
3 Sheff U	28	6	4	5	22	16	6	6	1	18	11	1.48	34
4 Preston	27	8	3	1	35	18	3	8	4	20	19	1.49	33
5 Liverpool	30	7	6	2	25	10	5	3	7	21	28	1.21	33
6 Bolton	28	7	3	4	22	16	5	3	6	18	21	1.08	30
7 Sheff W	29	8	4	2	27	11	1	7	7	13	26	1.08	29
8 Bury	26	7	4	3	24	14	2	5	5	12	23	0.97	27
9 Wolves	28	5	4	5	22	14	5	2	7	19	22	1.14	26
10 N Forest	30	8	3	4	30	16	1	5	9	14	33	0.90	26
11 Everton	26	6	1	5	30	22	5	2	7	19	28	0.98	25
12 W Brom	28	7	2	6	18	16	3	3	7	12	34	0.60	25
13 Blackburn	28	8	1	6	27	25	3	2	9	8	34	0.59	25
14 Sunderland	29	4	6	5	21	21	3	2	9	12	25	0.72	22
15 Stoke	28	6	3	4	25	18	3	0	12	18	41	0.73	21
16 Burnley	30	4	5	6	25	25	2	2	11	18	36	0.70	19

With three games remaining, Aston Villa were confirmed as Champions. More than that, they had become the first - and still the only - club to win the FA Cup and League title on the same day.

* * *

At ten past ten on the morning of Monday 12th April, a train carrying the Aston Villa team and officials pulled out of Euston Station, due to arrive in Birmingham at one o'clock. The details had been printed in Monday's papers and, consequently, a large crowd began to assemble in Queen Street at about midday. By the time the train was due in, the City Centre was at a standstill. Superintendents Beard, Thomas and Moore along with Inspectors Clark and Charlesly of the Birmingham Constabulary attempted to keep the platform clear but hundreds of fans swamped New Street Station taking up every available vantage point.

A massive cheer went up along with numerous hats as the train pulled into sight. A band struck up a rendition of 'See the Conquering Hero Comes'

as the claret and blue covered carriages screeched to a halt by the Queen Street exit. A char-a-banc should have been waiting but had yet to negotiate the mass of humanity which had thronged the roads around the station, all hoping to catch a glimpse of their idols. The committee and wives had to retreat back to their carriage from where Fred Rinder held aloft the English Cup to deafening cheers.

At last some vehicles, covered in the Club's colours of course, arrived to take the team on a tour of the City. John Devey took charge of the FA Cup whilst the Championship trophy was passed from player to wonderful player, each one receiving massive vocal encouragement from their fans below. The band continued to play as the procession moved off into Worcester Street. From there, it took in New Street, Colmore Row and Waterloo Street before halting momentarily out side the Old Royal in Temple Row. The manager of that establishment, Mr. McConville, congratulated the team and filled their Cup with champagne before the captain rose to address the masses.

John Devey thanked the people of Birmingham for their marvellous reception. He mentioned Lord Rosebery's comment about being a novice at football and continued: *"...and so I am a novice at speech making."* To the cheers of the crowd, he remarked about the grand game Everton had given his men and trusted that if ever Aston Villa were to be defeated by Everton in similar circumstances, they would accept their loss in the same sportsmanlike manner as the Liverpudlians.

It was time to move off again. Along Bull Street, down Snow Hill. Great Hampton Row. Temple Street. Summer Lane and Alma Street to Six Ways, Aston. All along the route the crowds loudly acclaimed the victors, waiving anything that came to hand. Finally, it was up Birchfield Road to the Old Crown and Cushion, for years the nerve-centre of Aston Villa Football Club. The strong association between Pub and Club was to end now that the Aston Lower Grounds were ready for occupation. How fitting that this relationship should bow out on the highest note possible.

The team dispersed, only to meet up again a few hours later for a banquet at the Old Royal, hosted by the directors of the Birmingham Hotel and Restaurant Company Limited. All the great and good of that exceptional City were on hand to honour Brum's magnificent sons. Aston Villa and the two trophies they had won it such breathtaking style had come home, and no better home could they have hoped to have.

The spoils of victory sat on the top table, property of the greatest football team ever assembled. A grand feast was laid on, the size of which may not have won the approval of Joe Grierson, but even with three games left in this extraordinary season, iron-hand Joe couldn't begrudge his charges their night of over-indulgence.

The waiters wore hunting coats with blue collars and cuffs in homage to the famous colours of the famous Football Club. Indeed, the whole room was a claret and blue heaven. One hundred and fifty guest danced the night away as they were entertained by a vocal group and a band.

There was a break for speeches. First, William and Edward Ansell handed over £25 to be divided between the winning team and their brilliant trainer. The President of the gathering, Mr. C.E. Mathews, gave each player a guinea before confessing that he had never been to a football match. He was given a taste of what he had missed by Mr. J. Ansell who led the assemblage on a trip down memory lane as he listed the grand achievements of Aston Villa FC. He said the Club had done as much as any temperance society to keep working men out of the public houses, although one supposes the Guv'nor at the Old Crown could have put him right there!

Finally, John Devey rose to speak. He had to wait for a full two minutes while the guests gave him and his men the noisiest standing ovation imaginable. He claimed, somewhat modestly, that the players had always tried to do their best and that they were motivated by an ambition to reach the top. He again paid tribute to Everton who had *"...played like men."*

* * *

Twenty-three years had passed since Messrs. Price, Scattergood, Hughes and Matthews had chatted in Heathfield Road. Twenty-one since George Ramsay launched himself on a group of churchmen and took them to Wellington Road. Seventeen years since the first major trophy success and the arrival of the great Archie Hunter. A decade had elapsed since the English Cup Competition was first conquered. A mere five years since the Villa flame flickered before Frederick Rinder called the Barwick Street meeting and breathed new life into the giant. Just three years since the League title had first been claimed. It seems such a short time in which Aston Villa had risen to football's greatest heights, achieved everything that could be achieved and spread their name throughout the planet.

The players deserved their night of celebration for they had proved themselves worthy of the Lion they were privileged to wear on their chests. In the space of four years, they had set a standard which Aston Villa would become accustomed to achieving and then surpassed themselves. Their whole-hearted commitment to the cause and the brilliance they displayed are what everyone who is ever fortunate enough to be in any way associated with the Club should aspire to. For only when one can stand equal to John Devey and his wonderful comrades can one deservedly claim the title 'Aston Villa Great'. It was not the trophies alone which mattered, although they are important enough. It was the grace with which they were won. It was the fact that the hard work which led to the success was not motivated by selfish concerns but by an unconditional love for the Club which came directly from the heart. That is what it means to be a Villaman and if, as in 1896/7, everyone at the Club evinces that love, then the football matches take care of themselves.

Aston Villa, Double Winners 1897. Back row (l-r) G.B. Ramsay (secretary), J. Grierson (trainer), H. Spencer, J. Whitehouse, J. Margoschis (chairman), A. Evans, J. Crabtree, J. Lees (director), C. Johnstone (director); front row (l-r) Dr. V.A. Jones (director), James Cowan, C. Athersmith, J. Campbell, J. Devey, F. Wheldon, John Cowan, J. Reynolds, F.W. Rinder (director). *Photo: Coloursport*

Chapter Twelve

The Football Business
George Ramsay and Frederick Rinder

If anyone could justifiably claim to have 'made' the Villa, then George Ramsay and Frederick Rinder - two gentlemen for whom the word 'great' does scant justice - are such men. What is beyond all shadow of a doubt is that between them they made Aston Villa great. It is hard to substantiate any claim that the Club would have scaled the heights it has without Ramsay and Rinder, quite simply because their like did not exist before them, they had no equals amongst their contemporaries, and no one has come close to matching their brilliance in the years since they journeyed to claret and blue heaven. It will not suffice to say they had no betters, for they performed on a far higher plain than anyone else in the field of sport.

We begin with the older of the two and the one who was first to make his mark on the Villa. It was 1855 that George Burrell Ramsay was born in Glasgow. It was there that, with modern football in its infancy, the little more than infant George first showed his amazing ability with the round leather. From as young as he could remember, Ramsay only ever wanted to do one thing: play football!

And boy was he good! A natural inside-forward, although he more frequently appeared at number 9, his exceptional close control saw him win numerous trophies in dribbling races. But he could, and did, play anywhere such was the God-given nature of his talent. He was even a gifted goalkeeper and could easily have displaced many top rank custodians. He was scientific in his methods of shot-stopping - an uncommon approach for that era.

As adulthood beckoned, he signed up for the Oxford club in his native land, still harbouring dreams of playing at the highest level. No doubt the newly instigated international matches had Ramsay yearning to represent his country. But, inexplicably, he never received offers to leave Oxford and so, at the age of 21, G.B.R. moved south. Thankfully for Aston Villa, his destination was Birmingham... and a place in history!

It was 1876 when the small Scotsman set up residence in the Second City. He had secured a clerical job at a firm of brassfounders and was soon on the lookout for teams of Brummagem ball-players who might offer him a game. First he had to overcome the language barrier though. So strong was Ramsay's accent that his new found friends had immense difficulty understanding him. All a far cry from days to come when everything the man said was listened to almost as if God himself were speaking.

George Ramsay

George got his first taste of English football in unexpected circumstances, when taking a stroll in Aston Park. A number of clubs trained and played matches in the grounds of Aston Hall, as well as on the football enclosure across the road where Nelson Road now runs. By an amazing stroke of luck, for which all modern day Villa fans should continually be thankful, the day Ramsay roamed it was the pioneering Wesleyans who were hoofing the orb. The Scotsman watched for a while and, noticing one of the 'elevens' was a man short, asked if he might join in.

The sad truth was that the Villa players were not very good. They had plenty of passion but the finer points of the game were lost on them. Not so with Ramsay though. Wearing a polo cap and long pants which he had made himself, he ghosted past tackles, dribbled the length of the pitch, scored marvellous goals and generally made his opponents look foolish during that 'debut'. He then proceeded to show them how it was done. His effect on the Christian Club was immediate. They begged him - though they didn't really have to - to join Aston Villa and immediately appointed him their captain, team selector and coach. William McGregor tells the story of that first meeting between man and Club:

"I have heard some of the old members speak of the fascination which Ramsay's dextrous manipulation of the ball... had for them. They had never seen anything like it. He had it so completely under control that it seemed impossible for them to tackle him. The members were ready to thrust all sorts of honours upon him, and he was literally compelled to take the captaincy."

Thus it was that Aston Villa stopped being a winter get-together for the members of a church cricket team and became a football club - one that would be feared and famed the world over. One of Ramsay's earliest gifts to the Club was the discovery of the Wellington Road enclosure. He spotted the unused meadow whilst on another of his strolls, this time with a friend named John Lindsay. A lease was duly agreed and Aston Villa had a home.

Now all they needed was a team to play and win there. That was Ramsay's next job. He did it - and continued to do it for nearly half a century - better than any man then or since. Of course, his greatest acquisition in those early days was Archie Hunter who, as we know, Ramsay snatched from under the noses of Calthorpe. By 1880, Aston Villa could boast a forward line of Andy Hunter, George Ramsay, Archie Hunter, Howard Vaughton and Eli Davis. All five were legends of the pre-League days and in combination were second only to the 1896/7 forwards for brilliance.

With such an awesome front rank, Villa cruised to their first major trophy success in 1880. Under the leadership of G.B.R. the Birmingham Senior Cup was won and the Club had become the top team in the West Midlands. From there it was a case of looking further afield in their quest for world domination. The FA Cup loomed as the next stepping stone to greatness, but it would have to be conquered without the on-field skills of George Ramsay. Injury forced him to retire and he handed the captaincy over to Archie Hunter before taking his place on the Committee, coaching and poaching players... in the nicest possible sense.

He may have been a player for only a short time (it was around his 25th birthday when he retired) but his impact was enormous. He played on a couple of occasions for the Birmingham FA and was unofficially Villa's first International, but it wasn't for Scotland. He was asked to play for the Welsh FA and lined up against a representative team from, of all places, Glasgow.

Ramsay had achieved much in his playing career, but it was nothing compared to what would follow after he hung up his boots. That said, the effect George the player had on the Villa should not be under-estimated. As William McGregor wrote: *"...it was George Ramsay who first moulded the style of the Club's play, and the Aston Villa team have never lost the reputation they gained for short, quick passing under Ramsay's direction."*

Ramsay added to his roll of duties in 1884 when he took the position of Club Secretary. He also added to Villa's list of brilliant footballers. His first dozen years on the Committee saw him bring in the likes of Arthur Brown, Jimmy Warner, Tom Riddell, Frank Coulton, Fred Dawson, Jack Burton, Albert Brown, Dennis Hodgetts, Harry Devey, Albert Allen, Gershom Cox, John Devey, Jas Cowan, Charlie Athersmith, and Billy Dickson - a veritable who's who of early association football. And, of course, the FA Cup was won in 1887. But by 1892, his hands had been tied by a Committee who were letting the Club down and lacked the vision to lead it to the pinnacle of the game. That was until Barwick Street of which we shall learn shortly.

Ramsay was a definite beneficiary of that infamous meeting. He remained as Secretary on the revamped Committee and set about building the Double team, this time with the help of fellow visionaries and without the hindrance of the less far-sighted. Fred Rinder looked after the finances required to lure the best players to Aston Villa, and George Ramsay was able to capture virtually any footballer he wanted. It was no longer necessary for him to batter his targets into submission by excessive use of his notorious charm and wit. The days of kidnapping the Hunters and Cowans of this world had gone forever.

Following Barwick Street, Ramsay found it increasingly difficult to carve the time to concentrate on the coaching side of his remit. Hence, Joe Grierson was brought in. The pressures of running the top professional League club in the land obligated George to give greater attention to the administration of Aston Villa, particularly as crowds - and the associated demands - grew. Yet he still made time to help in training and liked nothing better than a drink and a chat with the players and supporters. Despite the growing stature of the Club, Ramsay never distanced himself from the fans and was always present at benefit dinners and other get-togethers. Like William McGregor, no matter what he achieved and no matter what his job entailed, he never lost sight of the fact that he was a fan himself. The game was always more important than the result and the Club always came before personalities.

Ramsay continued his role of chief scout,

selector and secretary for a total of 42 years. This makes him the second longest serving 'manager' ever. His job and the way he executed it never changed in all that time, although the workload increased dramatically, to the detriment of his health. He simply didn't know when to stop and, particularly in the latter half of his four decade stint, he would occasionally be literally forced to take time off to recuperate and recharge his batteries. This he achieved by taking short breaks in Wales - a land he adored - always returning fired up and ready to fight for the Villa cause.

It should be remembered that he also held down a full-time job throughout his years as Club Secretary. His one major financial bonus from the Club came on 7th October 1911 when he was granted a benefit match. But, unlike players who received that honour, Ramsay's game was not a hastily arranged friendly. Instead, he was handed the gate money from the League match against Sunderland - which was watched by 28,000 spectators! Villa lost that game 3-1 and what is beyond all doubt is that George Ramsay would have given up every penny of his benefit to see that scoreline reversed.

He certainly deserved his bumper pay-day as a glance at his record of achievement highlights. As well as an incredible amount of local competition wins, under Ramsay's leadership Aston Villa won more League titles and FA Cups than any other club in England. They were unequalled during that era. Their position at the pinnacle of world football was a direct result of Ramsay's ability to get the right players for his team. Again, just a cursory glance at the list of men who donned the famous claret and blue jersey indicates the worth of G.B.R. to the Villa.

George Ramsay's last major foray into the transfer market was perhaps his greatest masterstroke of all and brought to the Club a player who only stayed for two and half years, but who enjoys a legendary status at Aston Villa comparable with any other footballer anywhere. Ten games into the 1919/20 season (the first campaign since the Great War) Villa found themselves rooted to the bottom of the table with just three points. It seemed that the unthinkable might happen and the greatest club in the world might actually get relegated.

The pessimists, though, reckoned without George Ramsay and his comrades who would not stand idly by and allow years of hard work and achievement to slip. Ramsay boarded a train for Barnsley and returned with a centre-half who was feared throughout the land. He had the worst disciplinary record of any player, counted condemned criminals amongst his closest friends and once carried a gun into contract negotiations. He was

also arguably the most fearsome and effective centre-half that ever lived. Frank Barson was his name and his effect on his new team-mates was immediate. In his first game for the Club, Middlesbrough were trounced 4-1 on their own patch. This started a run of ten wins from eleven games and saw Villa climb to mid-table respectability at the close of the campaign and, more importantly, win their sixth FA Cup.

When everyone panicked at Villa's plight early in 1919/20, Ramsay looked for the right player to stave off the impending disaster. He then quietly went about securing that player's services. That was Ramsay! As a contrast, when Villa finally did get relegated in 1936, the Committee (minus Ramsay) spent a small fortune buying a number of players in an attempt to avoid the drop. Ramsay achieved that aim with just one, carefully thought out acquisition.

When, in 1926, ill-health finally forced George Ramsay to relinquish the post of Secretary, he was made an honorary advisor to the Club and became a life vice-president. He took his seat in the stands and finally had the opportunity simply to enjoy the game. It was a sad day for both George himself and the Club he served so magnificently. He always missed the day-to-day involvement and the Villa could never find anyone to match Ramsay's administrative and footballing brilliance.

On 7th October 1935, an unbroken 59 year association with Aston Villa Football Club came to an end when George Ramsay passed away in Llandrindod Wells, his favourite holiday spot. It says on his gravestone, 'Founder of Aston Villa'. This is not strictly accurate for, as we know, he came to Brum two years after the Club was formed. Yet in another respect it is true. Aston Villa would probably not have survived without the good fortune of its Aston Park meeting with one of Scotland's finest sons. For it was he who took the Victorian equivalent of a pub team and turned them into a proper football club. He may not have been under the Heathfield Road gaslight, but he certainly created the Aston Villa which we know and love today. He even gave the Club its famous lion rampant crest and the legend 'Prepared'.

If there is a heaven, then George Ramsay has made his home in the bit of God's Kingdom which sits directly above the centre-spot at Villa Park. And every time the Claret and Blue takes to the hallowed turf, the loudest, most passionate cheer comes complete with a broad Glaswegian accent belonging to a football man, yes - but more than that: The Ultimate Villaman

* * *

A year after George Ramsay first arrived in Birmingham, another gifted administrator ventured south, though he didn't have as far to travel as Villa's Glaswegian genius. A 20 year old named Frederick W. Rinder left his native Liverpool in 1877 and, like his future associate, it was work rather than football which brought him to the rapidly expanding Midlands city.

Fred Rinder

It was not until 1880 that Fred stumbled across the Villa when he saw them march to Senior Cup glory. He became quite a regular at Wellington Road and in 1881 was granted membership of Aston Villa. The following year he was appointed to a post in the City Surveyors Office where he would spend the rest of his working career, giving a total of 40 years service to the City of Birmingham. During that time, he rose to the lofty position of Surveyor of Licensed Premises and Places of Amusement. This was more than just a mere title though. Rinder was charged with putting into practice Arthur Chamberlain's plan to reduce the number of pubs in Quaker-dominated Brum and he oversaw the building of cinemas at a time when they were springing up everywhere.

Rinder's day job is not something on which to dwell here. Suffice to say that implementing Birmingham's notoriously strict licensing laws and playing the major role in the growth of cinema in the City is worthy of a biography, regardless of the man's other achievements. The big question though is, with such a massive portfolio at the Surveyors Office, how on earth did Fred find the time to perform so outstandingly at the Villa? A confession is in order: This book will not even attempt to answer that one; rather, we can all simply marvel at this great man's stamina and ability. For, as we shall now see, Rinder's worth to Aston Villa has only been matched by George Ramsay. Not even the most lauded Villamen throughout the

Club's glittering history have had nearly as enduring an effect as Fred.

In 1886, Rinder was elected to the Villa Committee. His first year there could not have been more successful. On the pitch, the team won its first FA Cup. Although it may have been mere coincidence that Rinder's elevation came just twelve months before Archie Hunter led the side to victory, the 2-0 defeat of West Bromwich Albion at Kennington Oval certainly marked Fred's first year in style.

While the Cup was being won, the Committee's new boy had been successfully completing his first major task for the Club, the building of a new Grandstand at Wellington Road. It would not be the last time Rinder turned his attentions to stadium construction, but this first project produced a grand pavilion fit for the Champions of England. The finished article bore a slight resemblance to the Trinity Road Stand at Villa Park, more of which later.

The relatively successful late-1880's period, though, papered over cracks which were appearing at the Villa. A decent Cup run in 1888 was followed up by second place in the inaugural League season and all appeared to be going well. The truth was somewhat different, however, as the next two years showed. In 1890 Villa escaped the indignity of having to apply for re-election to the League they formed and a year later finished one place from bottom and only retained their position thanks to the expansion of the League to fourteen clubs. A very promising opening to the 1891/2 campaign was the prelude to a drop in form, at which point Rinder decided enough was enough. He could see that the Club was stagnating and realised that without strong leadership Aston Villa was more likely to go out of business than win trophies. The old gaslight was flickering but Rinder wasn't about to let it be extinguished.

By February 1892, Rinder had recruited enough support from Club members to call an extraordinary general meeting which was to be held at Barwick Street. Interestingly, 80 years later Doug Ellis used exactly the same methods to regain the Chair at Villa, but Barwick Street made Ellis's 1972 battle with Jim Hartley look like handbags at twenty paces.

Taking the floor and using his compelling oratory to maximum effect, Rinder launched a scathing attack on the tired old men who had let greatness slip away following the 1887 success. He called Aston Villa a shoddy organisation which allowed money to seep out of the coffers. This was said with particular reference to the lack of controls over admission payments, and the Committee's tormentor minced none of his words as he asserted that entrance money was not reaching the bank account.

The speech took the meeting by storm and the Committee were forced to resign en bloc. Under the Chairmanship of Issac Whitehouse and with Rinder as Financial Secretary and Ramsay retaining his position as Secretary, a new Committee was elected and pledged to make Aston Villa the greatest club in the world. Unlike the empty rhetoric of so many people who take control of football clubs, this promise was kept.

Several of the Wellington Road gatemen threatened to sue Rinder for slander over his allegations of fraud. Their threats were quickly dropped, however, when it was pointed out that no individuals had been named. Further, the irate workers would have been hard pressed to explain what followed. Rinder had twelve turnstiles installed at Perry Barr with the result that takings immediately rose from £75 to £250. And this was not as a result of a sudden increase in attendance!

Having shaken the Club out of its complacency, Rinder set about providing the finances for George Ramsay's team building. He also got involved in the odd signing himself, most notably with his trip down the coal mine to grab Steve Smith. In an earlier chapter, William McGregor's desire for a meaningful 'youth' policy was mentioned. It is worth noting the success of the development of raw talent at Villa, something which Rinder supervised. Over a period of twenty-five years, 23 international players were produced through Villa's reserve team. Remember, this was at a time when only three International games were played each season!

On the field the Club enjoyed unparalleled success and Rinder turned his attentions towards maximising its business potential. In 1896, the Aston Villa Football Club 'Limited' was formed with four directors - Joshua Margoschis, Charles Johnstone, James Lees and Fred Rinder, with Ramsay still Secretary. The Limited Company's first objective was to purchase the Aston Lower Grounds and build a new stadium on it. Rinder and Johnstone did most of the negotiations. Then Fred set about designing the finest football enclosure in the world. A year later and the Double winners were playing at what would eventually be renowned throughout the globe as Villa Park.

Despite all the expenditure involved in paying the leases on two grounds (Wellington Road and Villa Park) and building an entire stadium, when Rinder spoke to the 1897 Aston Villa AGM he announced record profits. These are detailed in a subsequent chapter but it is worth looking at one financial point from this marvellous season. As winners of the FA Cup, Villa received a little over a

tenth of the gate money collected at the semifinal and final stages of the competition. Rinder was not happy about this and opined that the FA should provide a more generous payout to the last four clubs in the competition. His words obviously struck a chord somewhere because when Villa next won the Cup in 1905, they received more than a third of the gate receipts from the semi's and final ties. Of course, the profits the FA make from charging high prices for the 'neutral ground' Cup ties are still the cause of much argument today.

With the Aston Lower Grounds ready for occupancy, an interesting thing occurred which gave a hint as to the depth of feeling Rinder had for the Villa. Some of the Club members proposed that, as Fred had designed the ground, the stadium - or at least part of it - should be named after him. Rinder was said to be filled with rage at such a suggestion and lectured the well-meaning members for fully twenty minutes on the great names associated with the Club. He said he would never dream of placing himself above people like Archie Hunter, George Ramsay, Dennis Hodgetts and a number of others The idea was quickly dropped although a similar idea was mooted when the Trinity Road Stand was completed in the 1920's. That too met with a very frosty response from the great man.

It was somewhat strange that Rinder should be so vehemently against his own immortalisation because he often came across as quite the egotist. He had a great belief in his own ability and could often bulldoze his way through objectors, showing little inclination to debate matters with others, preferring that people either agreed with and helped him, or shut up and got out of his way. Yet he was not so easily understood. He had a genuine desire to see Aston Villa be the best and always have the best. Anyone who shared that wish was immediately welcomed by Rinder and he would never step on someone else's territory. If another did their job well, Rinder would not seek to interfere.

His relationship with the players showed similar contradictions. Unlike Ramsay, Lees and McGregor, Fred was rarely one for mixing socially with the team or the supporters. He was, in fact, a fearsome disciplinarian and would not tolerate anything which fell below his own very high moral standards. The players had to follow the rules or expect censure.

Few Villa footballers ever dared cross swords with Fred Rinder. But the great Billy Walker wrote about an incident when one player did stand up to the (then) Chairman... and more than that, actually came out the winner! That player was Tommy Smart and his set to with Mr. Rinder involved his late arrival for a train taking the team to a match at

Newcastle. Rinder had a rule that the players should be on the platform twenty minutes before the train left. This applied to ALL away games. The allotted time came and went and Tommy was not to be seen. He eventually sprinted along New Street Station a mere two minutes before the train pulled out, having run all the way from Snow Hill. Billy Walker recorded what happened next:

"Rinder blasted: "What time's this Smart." "Just time to catch the train." Rinder ordered Smart to report to Villa Park and tell them he was in the reserves tomorrow. Smart said he'd been picked to play at Newcastle and that was where he was going."

Tommy Smart did play at Newcastle. In fact he was man of the match in a 1-0 win. Rinder congratulated the full-back after the match and said he'd try to forget what happened. Billy Walker claimed that no other player could have got away with such disobedience, and he was probably right. Even Frank Barson fell victim to Rinder's wrath on a number of occasions. Barson may have been one of the most feared men in the world in the 1920's, but he knew he couldn't push Rinder too far, although the two regularly argued.

Yet for all his toughness, Fred really cared for his players. Two incidents highlight this perfectly, the first again involved Frank Barson. In 1922, Villa sold Big Frank to Manchester United and promised their erstwhile centre-back rock a cut of the transfer fee. But the League Management Committee ruled that such a payment would be illegal because Barson had asked for a transfer. It would be quite natural to assume that the Villa wouldn't be too concerned with that decision as, after all, it would save the Club some money. But Fred Rinder believed that the promise to his player should be kept and presented Barson's case in person to the Management Committee. It was to no avail but it showed that Rinder was prepared to go out on a limb for his men.

The other incident which deserves mention could be said to have won Villa the FA Cup. 15 minutes into the 1913 Final against Sunderland, Clem Stephenson was brought down in the box. Villa's outside-right, Charlie Wallace took the spot kick but sent it wide. As the players came off at halftime, the winger was distraught, so much so that he wouldn't talk to anyone. Enter Fred Rinder who sat with Wallace throughout the interval, first consoling him and then picking him up for the second half. Towards the end of the game, Wallace sent over a corner which Tom Barber headed home for the only score of the match and Villa won their fifth FA Cup.

That 1913 Cup Final came in Rinder's 21st year on the Villa Board and the players said it was their intention to win the Double to help him celebrate. They narrowly missed out by finishing second to Sunderland in the League, but their desire to 'win for Rinder' showed how much respect and regard they had for the man.

It was also in 1913 that Fred Rinder's latest plans to expand Villa Park were passed by the shareholders. He envisaged a 130,000 ground capacity, but at that time it was a more modest 103,000 which would be the immediate aim. Had it been realised, Villa could have banked £4,000 (at 1913 prices) for each full house. Sadly, the War put paid to those plans and whilst the ground did eventually exceed an 80,000 capacity, Fred's grand design never materialised.

Things were never quite the same at the Club following the end of the Great War. The reason was that the newer shareholders were simply not on the same wavelength as the older men who had nurtured the Villa into the game's biggest giant. In 1921, there was an unsuccessful attempt to oust Rinder from the Board. It was alleged that he had been involved in suspect share deals and his attacks on other members of the Club's management made him unpopular in some quarters.

But Fred survived the attempted coup and soon threw himself into further ground development. 1922 saw the start of the construction of the Rinder designed Trinity Road Stand. Until then, Witton Lane had been the main stand at Villa Park. The new construction, though, was to outshine all other structures at sports enclosures the world over. So beautiful was Rinder's design that it now enjoys listed building status and harmonises perfectly with Sir Thomas Holte's 17th Century family seat across the road: Aston Hall. To this day, no other stadium can boast such an architectural masterpiece.

It wasn't just the exterior that stood out either. In the depths of the building were oak-panelled rooms and the changing rooms were better than anything else in the world, offering every possible comfort to the players.

There was also a state-of-the-art X-ray room to aid the speedy diagnosis of injuries. And, as a testament to Rinder's vision, the Trinity Road Stand included the first restaurant at any football ground. The idea was that Villa Park should be more than just a stadium.

The Stand could never be called ostentatious, but it did reflect Villa's status as the biggest and best football club on the planet. This is what the Club had to say about their new construction in 1924:

"...the new pavilion presents quite a noble

appearance, and has been erected at a very considerable cost. The aim of the Directors has been to make the people who visit the match comfortable rather than with the idea of any great profit accruing from the enterprise. Having taken one of the leading positions of the Association football clubs of the kingdom, the Aston Villa directorate have decided that they will be socially in the van as well as being among the front rank in the field of sport."

They weren't joking about the cost. The final bill was a well over-budget £90,000 and the shareholders went for Rinder's jugular as a result. They criticised such an enormous outlay while Fred claimed that, apart from the fact that the Villa deserved the best, such a fine building and the facilities therein would see the Club benefit in the long-term. But the shareholders neither possessed Rinder's visionary excellence nor did they want to listen to anything he had to say. Further, via a certain amount of massaging of figures, they claimed that the cost of the Stand threatened Villa's very existence. Not for the first, nor last, time in the Club's history, tales of imminent financial collapse were grossly exaggerated to benefit those with an eye on power.

Fred Rinder saw his position was hopeless and resigned his seat on the Board. Before he left he warned friends that the people who were gaining control of the Club were far worse than the men he ousted at Barwick Street and would only succeed in ripping the heart out of Aston Villa. He left with the words: *"Finance is important but one should never forget that we are not talking about a mere business. This is THE Aston Villa Football Club and it deserves nothing short of the best. I hope and pray the new brood can give it that."*

They couldn't. The Villa were never the same after that. To the present day, the Club has never come close to the success and status it enjoyed in Rinder's years. From 1924 it was downhill all the way. The early 1930's saw Villa twice finish runners up in the League, but that papered over the cracks just as the years preceding Barwick Street had. The unthinkable finally occurred in 1936 when Aston Villa were relegated. In Birmingham, grown men cried with despair, unable to comprehend what had happened. Elsewhere, to say the football world was shocked would be an understatement. It took a long time for people to accept that the great Aston Villa would really be playing in Division Two.

There was only one answer to the Villa's plight. The Club had been run into the ground by the shareholders who could not follow the lead of Fred Rinder. Now those same men knew what they had to do - call for the one man who could save the Lions. Resultantly, Howard Spencer selflessly stepped down to make room on the Board for Fred Rinder.

At the grand age of 79, he breezed through the Villa Park gates and breathed new life into the Club. But he didn't seek revenge on those who had hounded him out a dozen years earlier. Nor did he attempt to take complete control of the Villa. Instead, he did what had served him so well in the glory days and sought the right people to do the work that was necessary to return the Club to greatness. With this in mind, he went on a quest for a man to replace Villa's first manager, the departed Jimmy McMullen. Rinder brought to the Club a legend amongst managers, the man who is credited with developing continental football to such a level that the Europeans overtook the British. Jimmy Hogan was his name. With Rinder at the helm and Hogan playing the 'Ramsay' role, everything was geared for a return to the golden era. World domination Mk. II seemed just round the corner.

It took two seasons but Villa did return to the top flight - as Champions. The team Hogan built was considered to be of such quality that it ranked with Devey's charges of 40 years earlier. Indeed, even today, those people who saw them believe the Villa have not produced a better team to the present day. Sadly, the Second World War prevented that side from fulfilling its potential, and by the time peace returned, the great Villa leaders were gone.

Fred Rinder did not survive to the outbreak of War. On 19th December 1938 he watched a reserve match and returned to his home in Somerset Road, Edgbaston, where he had a seizure. He lasted until Christmas Day when he died aged 81.

Four days later, what can only be described as football's equivalent of a State Funeral took place at Harborne Parish Church. Pretty much every major name ever connected with Aston Villa were there and his pall bearers were Claret and Blue legends Frank Barson, Billy Walker, Jimmy Allen, Alex Massie, Eric Houghton and Frank Broome.

Most football clubs and organisations were represented. At the time of his death Rinder was a senior vice-president of the Football League and his send off was befitting one of the game's great rulers. And all the football people mingled with some of the highest ranking Freemasons in Britain. They came to honour their brother, for Rinder was a Past Master of the Bedford Lodge. The entrance to the Church was lined with footballers on one side and Masons on the other. Finally, the City of Birmingham mourned one of its great administrators. Quite simply, regardless of football allegiances, Frederick Rinder touched every Brummie in one way or another. He gave them cinema, took away a few of their pubs, helped with numerous local charities and ensured that the City could boast the world's finest football club.

Following a death, there should really be a celebration of a great man's life. But, from a Villa point of view, there was further sadness with the departure of Fred Rinder. The man who took over Fred's directorship was Norman Smith. Villa fans who can remember the 1960's will know that it was under Smith's chairmanship that the Villa stared bankruptcy in the face as the Club dived towards the Third Division. This is not meant as an attack on Smith alone, but it highlights perfectly the difference between the truly great Aston Villa and the post-Rinder era. Only the European Cup win of 1982 would meet with Frederick Rinder's approval. But he would have built on it and ensured that the trophy had virtually a permanent home at Villa Park. To sum up, Rinder and the Club he ran refused to countenance the notion of failure during their happy and fruitful union.

The 1897 FA Cup Final in progress at Crystal Palace

Chapter Thirteen

Fortress Villa
Wellington Road and Villa Park

Don't attempt to look for it. Sadly it isn't there any more. But should anyone wish to take a trip down memory lane, a few directions may be in order. Start at the Perry Barr roundabout. The Old Crown and Cushion is still there, but it is an ugly modern building nowadays. Its only connections with better times are its name and the fact that it stands on in the exact spot where Villa made their headquarters from 1876-97. One would, however, never guess the nature of its great history, nor indeed that it had one.

So leave the pub behind and start walking down Wellington Road. The first turning on the left is Leslie Road. This marks one edge of a famous old enclosure. Continue along Wellington Road to the next turning, Willmore Road. Directly opposite this street used to stand a blacksmith's yard which, as we shall find out, was a significant sporting landmark of the late-Victorian period. The road itself ploughs a course straight down the middle of Aston Villa's first permanent stadium. Those with a vivid imagination should take a walk down Willmore and let the mind act as a time machine. It is still possible to feel a strong passion and pride about the place.

George Ramsay and John Lindsay ventured on a similar journey in 1876. Their football club had played matches in Wilson Road (Birchfield), Aston Park and on the football enclosure at the northern edge of the Aston Lower Grounds Pleasure Park. It had always been a case of find a green area and mark up a pitch. Now, they needed something more: a permanent base from which to launch their quest for glory.

Perry Barr was all a bit different then. It was a tiny village, waiting to be swallowed up by its rapidly expanding neighbour, Birmingham. There was even a toll gate on Birchfield Road, a vital source of income for the sleepy hamlet. Little did the villagers realise that it would soon become a mecca for football fans the land over. William McGregor explained what Ramsay and Lindsay found whilst on their wee constitutional:

"It (Wellington Road) was a capital field, although when the Villa took it there was a hayrick not far from the centre of the ground, a number of trees along the touchlines, a pool not far away, and a nasty hill near the lefthand corner of the top goal. It was not an ideal enclosure, by any means; but it was quite good enough for those days."

Football grounds certainly weren't stately homes in the 1870's, but it took a special kind of imagination to look at a rather rough meadow in a small village and recognise the potential for a grand stadium. But the Villa had had enough of waste grounds and parks pitches, so they settled for what they could afford and leased their first home. Ramsay immediately found the tenant butcher/farmer who held the lease on the pasture. They struck up a deal whereby the Club paid £5 per annum for their field of dreams. The Members worked tirelessly to transform the area into a fit playing surface, although the trees along the one side remained for a while. They provided welcome shelter (and something to lean on) for spectators.

On 30th September 1876, the grand opening occurred - except it wasn't particularly grand! The visitors on that historic day were Wednesbury Town. The crowd numbered a highly respectable... 21. Each paid three'pence, making the Villa's first gate a much needed 5/3 (26.25 pence). That said, those first fans had also to meet the Perry Barr toll gate levy. They also had a chance to spend money in the ground. Ever the visionaries, Ramsay and McGregor had sold a franchise to a local refreshment vendor. For a small fee, the trader brought his horse and stall into the enclosure and kept the crowd fed and watered, and his profits up.

The ground didn't change much in its early years. Little bits of temporary construction here and there including an area set aside for horses and carriages. This encouraged the more affluent Brummies to come and see the Villa. Crowds rose steadily, thanks first to the fascination which George Ramsay's skills held for sports fans, and then the immense pulling power of the great Archie Hunter. The Villa were becoming one of the most attractive sides in the land and one could be sure of a fine demonstration of the art of football at Wellington Road.

It wasn't until 1886 that the first major alteration to the ground came about. Newly elected to the Committee, Fred Rinder designed a grandstand for Wellington Road and oversaw its construction. The structure, which was similar in appearance to the later Trinity Road Stand at Villa Park, was one of the finest stands in the country and attracted numerous new supporters, particularly in deepest winter. Still, most of the crowd were at the mercy of the elements but for a little extra admission fee, fans could enjoy the most comfortable surroundings in football.

One thing the grandstand didn't have, however, was changing rooms. It had been proposed that they should be included, but it was decided that the Blacksmith's Yard across Wellington Road satisfied the Villa's needs. Indeed, the Yard provided very good facilities for the era, so much so that Birchfield Harriers athletic club also utilised that area as their dressing rooms.

The combination of a fine enclosure and the best team in the region caused supporters to bear down on Perry Barr, as the City to the south was mirroring. The increased gates were not lost on the tenant farmer who first upped the Villa's annual rent to £8 and then £10. It seemed that the cost was set to keep rising, but the Club had no security from the agreement. So the Committee approached the owners of the the land, the Bridge Trust School. A three year lease was obtained at a yearly rent of £60. The cost had shot up, but it was a small price to pay for stability.

Another price which had to paid was admission. 1892 and Barwick Street resulted in the installation of twelve turnstiles at Wellington Road. It didn't affect attendances - in fact they rose as the team improved. But some fans would go to enormous lengths to avoid paying their sixpence entrance. On matchday, the water tower behind the Steam Tram Depot (situated on what is now the corner of Birchfield and Willmore Roads) would be covered with budding mountaineers who scaled the heights to get a free view of the Villa doing likewise.

By this time, the ground had a capacity of 27,000, and nearly that many had watched Villa in an FA Cup tie against Preston in 1888 (the Perry Barr record). All a far cry from the 21 fans who first entered the ground and the days when only William McGregor and George Ramsay's brother would constitute the crowd. With such a rise in interest in Aston Villa, the Committee were desperate to develop Wellington Road. They approached the Bridge Trust, whose attitude was similar to that of the farmer who first leased the enclosure to the Club. The earlier £60 per year had doubled and eventually the owners demanded a rent of £200. But the final straw for the Villa came when the Bridge Trust refused to assist with even the basic maintenance of the site, let alone help with the expansion of the stadium.

A new home was required and, if it's a stadium you want, Fred Rinder's your man. He cast his alert eye down Aston Lane and espied the Aston Lower Grounds Pleasure Park. But before plans could be made for a move, the finance had to be in place. There was only one realistic way to achieve this, so Aston Villa became a Limited Company at the beginning of 1896. In total, 2,000 shares were issued at £5 each, of which 1,772 were immediately applied for. Following the issue there were 803 shareholders, including 296 who had previously been unconnected with the Club. Obviously the Villa were seen as a good investment. This belief would have been strengthened by a look at the original Board members: Fred Rinder, Joshua Margoschis, Charles Johnstone and James Lees, with George Ramsay as Secretary. These men of great vision and ability would oversee the spending of the near £10,000 capitalisation. All very different from a mere 22 years earlier when sixteen Wesleyans paid one shilling each to form Aston Villa F.C.

But before we consider the great construction which was going on in Aston while the Villa team stormed to Double glory, there is still the matter of the final days at Wellington Road. And what days they were. April 1896 saw the Championship come to Perry Barr along with three lesser trophies. This was followed by the matches we have just learned about. Yet when the first team played their last match on their famous sloping pitch, they were still to win a competition in 1897. But when they took the field for their first home League game at the Aston Lower Grounds, they were Division One Champions and FA Cup Winners. The Double was the parting gift to the Wellington Road enclosure, a ground from where Aston Villa plotted their course to the pinnacle of world sport. It was understandable then that William McGregor should say: *"It was a wrench for some of the old school to be divorced from Wellington Road, but there can be no doubt that the Villa acted wisely when they launched their great Aston scheme..."*

On Good Friday 1897, Villa reserves took on their Shrewsbury counterparts in a Birmingham and District League match. The very next day, Villa Park opened. It was a decidedly low-key end to 21 glorious years. As Birmingham expanded, so the meadow-turned-stadium was swallowed up as Leslie and Willmore Roads became home to working Brummies. One wonders how many residents of those streets realise exactly what an incredible history of achievement is buried beneath their abodes.

* * *

Setting the controls of our time machine back a little, we travel to pre-Civil War days: The 1630's to be more precise. At the time, Sir Thomas Holte was building himself a palatial home called Aston Hall. Down the slope on the east side of this magnificent construction lay an area of flat land which would become known as, first the Aston Lower Grounds and, later Villa Park. Back in the 17th Century, Holte's staff used to play a form of football on the exact spot where today's claret and blue heroes ply their trade. And to think Wembley claims to be the sport's spiritual home!

By the mid-Victorian epoch, the Aston Lower Grounds Pleasure Park sprang up. For a while it was one of Birmingham's biggest attractions. Where the Witton Lane Stand now extends was a sub-tropical garden. The Holte End replaced a magnificent lawn and flower beds. The Villa Park pitch used to be an ornamental lake and aviary and the Witton End was once home to a landscaped flower garden and highly ornate fountain. Where the old Lions Club was housed used to be a bowling green, tennis courts and rifle range, while the Villa Village shop site was a theatre attached to an aquarium (which became the Club's offices) and a restaurant.

The Pleasure Park was huge. Even Witton Road didn't contain its expanse. A boating lake sat on the Perry Barr side of that thoroughfare. But, most importantly of all for we sports fans, an all purpose enclosure provided a home to cricket, football and athletics at the north-west corner of the Park, approximately where Nelson Road now runs.

It was on this enclosure that the old Birmingham Cricket and Football Club (no relation to Small Heath FC) played home matches. WG Grace played cricket there on numerous occasions. Buffalo Bill hosted his Wild West Show in the enclosure (and complained that attendances were adversely affected by the Villa up at Perry Barr). And, returning to cricket, Australia once defeated an England side in under six hours at Aston.

By the 1890's, however, the Pleasure Park was on its last legs. The crowds had diminished and the buildings had seen better days. The Aston Lower Grounds were obviously ripe for development, but even so it took one hell of a vision to picture the biggest and grandest football stadium blossoming from the flower beds and lakes.

Fred Rinder, as we should all be aware, possessed such vision. He and Charles Johnstone approached the owners of the site, Flowers Brewery, and negotiated a brilliant deal for the Villa. This was confirmed at a shareholders meeting in the Collonade Hotel in May 1896. The Club had secured a 21 year lease on the Lower Grounds at an annual rental of £300, which included rates and taxes up to £75 p.a. with any additional amount split *50/50* with Flowers. But, best of all, Rinder and Johnstone secured the right to buy the land at a fixed rate of £5 per square yard at any time over the following 21 years. When the Villa took up this offer in 1911, the value of that forward thinking was realised in more ways than one.

But that was all to come. As soon as the deal was struck, work began on what would be Villa Park. So quickly did the stadium take shape that matches could have been played there at the start of the 1896/7 season although attendances would have been small as the stands were still mere shells. The ground had taken shape enough, though, for the *Birmingham Daily Post* to comment on 4th May 1896 that the Lower Grounds: *"...should become a grand enclosure, but it will be a long time before it equals the field at Perry Barr."* Perhaps not as long as they thought!

The pitch had been laid almost a year before the first ball was kicked on it. It was smaller than today's hallowed rectangle, measuring 100 by 70 yards (now 115 x 72). Final work on the green by Mr. Bates, the Warwickshire Cricket Club groundsman, ensured it was in pristine condition. Running round the pitch was a quarter mile long, 24 feet wide, cycle track - one of the fastest and best in the land. Cycling was a well supported sport a century ago, but Birmingham was without a good enough arena to attract the top competitions. The Villa Board put that right.

The oval stadium which rose above the track was a genuine Goliath. 50,000 tonnes of soil were needed to form the banks of the enclosure and 200 tonnes of iron were used to construct the grandstands abreast each touchline.

Along Witton Lane was the main stand, the middle portion of which provided seating reserved for shareholders. Towards the Holte Hotel end of the Witton Lane Stand there were 5,500 seats whilst the other end housed 4,500 standing spectators. In addition, there was a covered terrace running the whole length of the pitch at the front of the grandstand.

Witton Lane also included offices, and dressing rooms for both footballers and cyclists. The Villa changing room was the best ever seen anywhere. It included a Turkish bath, vapour chamber and a plunge bath said to be large enough to learn to swim in.

The rest of the ground was all terraced, with admission costing a mere sixpence. The banks behind the goals stood 23 tiers deep, as did the steps on the Trinity Road side. Here, a 100 yard-long stand protected the 'working class' supporters from the elements. By combining cheap prices with a few comforts, the Villa Board ensured that Villa's 'core' support grew rapidly and the mid-Winter games did not see poor weather adversely affecting attendances. That was how administrators thought a hundred years ago. However, there were to be no more 'free' vantage points like the old Perry Barr Water Tower. Massive billboards embraced each end of the ground, obscuring the view of even the most agile tree-climber!

Alterations were made to the Holte Hotel with its accommodation expanded greatly. James Lees took over the management of the building which would, in time, become home to young players taking their first steps on the way to claret and blue stardom.

Further innovations included areas for supporters to store their bicycles safely during the match; plenty of refreshment bars situated all round the stadium, and numerous entrances and exits to aid safe welcoming and dispersal of the 50,000 initial capacity.

* * *

Thus it was that the world's greatest sporting arena was born. Truly, there was nothing like it anywhere. Perry Barr, which served the Club so well for 21 years and had become famed the globe over, was no more. Its successor was a magnificent enclosure which soon attained a special atmosphere of its own. So much so, in fact, that the great Billy Walker would later write:

"About Villa Park itself hung an aura that seems almost visible. Most certainly it is there to be felt and I know of no other ground, with the exception of Hampden, that has the same effect on one. Almost it seems to be peopled by ghosts, amiable ghosts whose job it is to breath the great Villa spirit into generation after generation of ambitious youngsters who pass through the great gates to achieve a life's ambition to wear the famous claret and blue of the great club."

The first of those future ghosts of glory past would take to the awe-inspiring stadium on Saturday 17th April, 1897 - exactly one week after those same eleven had secured the Double. This was the perfect marriage of the world's greatest footballers and a home befitting their stature.

Chapter Fourteen

All Good Things...

It was a Saturday, approaching 3 o'clock, and in those pre-TV days that meant only one thing: Football! The season was drawing to a close. The Villa had won the Double. Their opponents, Blackburn Rovers, were lying close to the foot of the table but were certain to avoid the dreaded Test Matches.

The fact that there was nothing but pride to play for would normally have been enough to lower the crowd drastically. Add to that the fact that the weather on 17th April was horrendous in the extreme, and a crowd of 3,000 would have been about right in normal circumstances.

But these weren't normal circumstances. The world's finest stadium was about to be christened and 15,000 braved the elements to be able to say a collective 'I was there'. Included in that number was an enormous contingent from Lancashire who had travelled down on two specially chartered trains to play their part in the grand opening.

The stadium was not yet complete. There was still a little work to be done on the Witton Lane side while the roofing on Trinity Road had not quite been finished. Further, the expected final capacity of 70,000 would not be reached until the start of the '97/8 season, but with the ground already able to hold 50,000, the Lower Grounds actually looked quite empty on its big day. Still, those that were there took the opportunity to thoroughly investigate Villa's new home.

For a while, it was not certain that the match would go ahead, so vicious was the rain assaulting Birmingham. Eventually, though, the claret and blue eleven appeared from the Witton Lane tunnel to an ear-bursting cheer.

Blackburn lost the toss, and a tradition was born with Villa spending the first half defending what would eventually become the famous and awesomely mammoth Holte End. Right to the present day, whenever this custom is not followed, boos greet the opposing captain who has dared to go against history.

Right from the off it was obvious that Rovers were no match for a Villa team who, conscious of the importance of the occasion, played as if the Championship was at stake. It took just six minutes for the home side to open the scoring through a brilliant solo effort by John Campbell. In all likelihood, no better goal has ever been scored in 100 years of football at the Midlands' Mecca.

Campbell received the ball on the halfway line and embarked on a 35 yard run which took him past no less than five opponents before unleashing a thunderous shot which zipped into the far corner of the Witton End net. It was a goal much like Dalian Atkinson's famed 1992 effort at Wimbledon, with a less nonchalant finish but a better build-up. Not surprisingly, the crowd were ecstatic, but it was noted that they went wild in a way rarely seen in Victorian England. Indeed, the celebrations for Queen Victoria's Diamond Jubilee that year could not begin to compete with the roar which greeted that history-making strike.

Villa continued to press, their exhibition football leaving their opponents chasing shadows much of the time. The half-backs fed the forwards brilliantly whilst the front five knocked the ball about with a flowing style which only the Villa could produce.

One moment of complacency, however, almost led to Rovers writing their own page in Villa's history. Proudfoot - the one visitor who really got to grips with the game - created an opening for Nicholls who poked the ball into the goal. He was judged offside though, and thus denied the first strike at the Holte.

But that attack apart, it was all Villa. Both John and Jas Cowan had good efforts dealt with by Rovers' 'keeper, Ogilvie, as did John Devey. The pressure eventually paid dividends as half-time approached. Fred Wheldon let fly from 30 yards out. As the ball shot towards goal, Killean tried to intercept. It is the subject of some speculation whether he got a touch on it or not, but if he did it wasn't enough to change the trajectory and Wheldon's thunderbolt hit the back of the net. Some record books credit this as an own goal, but contemporary reports accredit Wheldon. Meanwhile, Killean's moment of ignominy would come in the second period. Despite the debate over the actual scorer, Wheldon would later claim his place in the record books by scoring the first ever hat-trick at Villa Park in the victory over

Sheffield Wednesday on the opening day of the following season, a feat he repeated three days later against West Brom!

The second half of Villa Park's inaugural match began in the same vein as the first, with the home side bearing down on their visitors. Most disturbingly for Rovers, Villa's right wing was beginning to shine

Ogilvie and his backs did well to hold out, however, and it took some time before the Holte End net embraced the ball. Again, Villa's third score is the subject of certain confusion in record books. John Cowan is credited nowadays with that strike, which is somewhat surprising as Campbell was in fact the man who shot for goal. But not even the Villa Number '9' can claim it, because his low drive was turned into the net by none other than Killean. Thus it was that the first goal in front of the famous terrace was an own goal by a Blackburn Rovers full-back.

The fans certainly had their moneys worth on that historic day. Villa ran out comfortable winners playing with the style and dash for which they were known the world over. The players who first tasted the glory of treading that most hallowed of turfs were:

Aston Villa: Whitehouse, Spencer, Evans, Reynolds, Jas Cowan, Crabtree, Athersmith, Devey, Campbell, Wheldon, John Cowan.

Blackburn Rovers: Ogilvie, Brandon, Killean, Booth, Crampton, Anderson, Nicholls, Hargreaves, Proudfoot, Wilkie, Campbell.

Referee: Mr. F. Bye (Sheffleld).

* * *

A mere forty-eight hours passed before Villa Park next hosted a contest, and it was a day of both glory and tragedy. Before Wolves became the ground's second visitors, the 50,000 attendance watched the Sport & Play Cycling Tournament featuring an international line-up of some of the fastest men on two wheels.

An otherwise highly successful meeting was marred by a serious accident involving a crowd favourite, A.W. Harris. After about three miles of a ten mile scratch race, part of Harris' bike gave way causing the rider to be thrown from his machine with horrific force. He was knocked unconscious and sustained a fractured skull. At 5 a.m on 21th April, Harris died in the General Hospital as a result of his injuries.

This obviously took the shine off an otherwise glittering afternoon, when the largest attendance ever at a League match saw Aston Villa give one of the greatest performances in their illustrious history, totally outclassing their Black Country rivals.

Crabtree was injured; thus Frank Burton was re-called to the side. Wolves, meanwhile, were at full-strength. The visitors won the toss and immediately broke the tradition by choosing to defend the Holte End. Okay, so perhaps one game maketh not a custom, but Wolves were made to pay for their folly all the same.

Straight from the kick-off, Campbell pinpointed the speeding Athersmith down the right. His cross found John Cowan who had all the time and space in the world to pick his spot for a dream start. Sadly, the spot Cowan picked was the wrong side of the upright.

On five minutes, after Reynolds had been just too high with a terrific long-range effort, Cowan redeemed his earlier miss and became the first Villa man to score at the Holte. Athersmith began the move with an exhilarating run. The ball was laid inside to Campbell who drew the full-back before knocking a square ball inside to Cowan. His neat side foot nestled into the corner of the net for one-nil.

Wolves, playing with the wind, tested the Villa with a couple of freekicks, one of which saw Spencer head clear from under the crossbar. But the hosts were soon back in their stride. Campbell tried a carbon copy of his opener against Blackburn, this time beating four opponents only for his powerful shot to clear the bar.

Wheldon carried the ball half the length of the field before picking out Jas Cowan who narrowly missed the target. Jas then repeated his near-miss following a brilliant interchange between Athersmith and Devey down the right which had sliced through Wanderers' defence like a hot knife through butter. The visitors too had their moments with Whitehouse called upon to make three fine saves. But it was Villa's flying outside right who really caught the eye. Charlie was up for this game and there was nothing (or at least nothing in the rulebook) the poor Wolves backs could do to halt him.

Villa came out for the second half a goal to the good and with the elements in their favour - a devastating combination made all the more daunting by the fact that they were ready to step up a few gears. They immediately attacked and within a minute of the re-start, skipper John Devey beat Tenant to double his side's advantage.

On fifty minutes, John Cowan vent on a mazey solo run before cutting in from the Trinity Road side and firing into the bottom right hand corner.

Then Owen had a good effort for Wolves before Howard Spencer was bitten by the dribbling bug. He carried the ball out of defence (unheard of at every other ground in the country) beating four players before a fifth brought him down illegally.

Shortly after, Villa's right-wing pair again tore through the Wolves defence to set up John Campbell with the easiest of tap-ins. Burton, Wheldon and Reynolds all stung Tenant's hands whilst Wolves' rare sorties into enemy territory found the home backs in fine form.

The icing on the cake came five minutes from time. A lovely piece of trickery from Campbell created enough space for the Scotsman to strike an absolute beauty from 15 yards to produce a final, and decidedly deserved, result of 5-0.

* * *

Villa Park (or the Aston Lower Grounds) had only been open three days, yet two different sports had showcased there. A further two days on in the life of that great stadium saw a third. The Old Villans Club hosted their Annual Sports and Athletics Event at the ground. The old-timers got a taste of the Villa's new home by taking part in both 100 yards and 220 yards flat handicaps which saw the great Howard Vaughton and John Devey's Uncle Harry in top form.

Then it was the turn of the current players to get their running boots on. In the heats, Tom Wilkes defeated John Campbell; Powderhall man Jas was - much to his annoyance - outpaced by Fred Wheldon, while Albert Evans got the better of reserve team player J. Field. But the shock came in the last heat where John Cowan held on to 2 of his 9½ yards start over Charlie Athersmith to make it into the final. Incredibly enough, out of a playing squad littered with speed merchants, it was goalkeeper Wilkes who emerged triumphant from the meeting.

A successful afternoon of athletic pursuits led to an evening of merriment as the Old Villans held their Annual Dinner at the Old Royal in the City. William McGregor presided over events, joined on the top table by Fred Rinder, James Lees, Charles Johnstone and Howard Vaughton. One would have thought that the team's recent success would be praised to the rafters, but it was merely stated that the Double was in keeping with the traditions of Aston Villa. This classic understating of a marvellous achievement could be seen as displaying arrogance, yet it does serve to show just how dominant the Club were in the 1890's.

* * *

Villa interest was split between the Lower Grounds and the famous Ibrox Stadium on 24th April. At the former, Villa had to field an unfamiliar line-up against Walsall in the final of the Mayor of Birmingham's Charity Cup. The team changes were forced on the selectors because three regulars had to travel to Glasgow to represent the Football League against their Scottish counterparts

Howard Spencer, John Devey and Charlie Athersmith were the three who added to their haul of 1897 honours. Devey began the game at centre forward, and it has to be said he didn't look good there. At half-time, he swapped places with Steve Bloomer. The Derby man fared no better down the middle but, with Devey linking up with Charlie on the right, the English forwards enjoyed a better second half. It was the Scots, though, who ran out comfortable 3-0 winners - so comfortable that reports claimed they would have hit double figures but for the brilliance of Spencer who was universally acclaimed as man-of-the-match.

Back in Aston, the home team looked like this:

Whitehouse, Welford, Evans, Reynolds, Jas Cowan, Burton, Steve Smith (switching from his usual left-wing role), Harvey, Campbell, Wheldon, John Cowan.

Despite the fact that the above eleven had never played together before, they should still have coasted to victory against their vastly inferior opponents. Unsurprisingly however, Villa took things easy and viewed the game as little more than a practice session.

For the first ten minutes, Walsall found themselves completely outplayed and Wheldon's goal from a Smith centre should have been the cue for the floodgates to open. But for the rest of the half, all Villa had to show for their dominance was a series of hopelessly misdirected shots, Jas Cowan being the worst offender of all.

The second half opened with the home team strolling around, putting on a bit of a show for the crowd who had turned up for this, the centrepiece of the Birmingham Charity Festival. Walsall, for their part, started to take things much more seriously to the extent that Copeland punished Villa's complacency with a fine header from a left wing cross.

This stirred Villa into action and Smith wasted a good chance before John Cowan saw a shot cleared off the line. Wheldon managed to get in two long-range efforts in quick succession, both of which smashed off the crossbar. The match closed without further score. Six days later, the teams replayed. Jimmy Whitehouse was carried off with an injury early in the game and 10-man Villa lost out 2-1.

Before Villa had a chance to suffer defeat at the hands of Walsall, there was the small matter of the last League match of the season. On 26th April the team travelled to fourth placed Preston on a windy Monday afternoon where a paltry 3,000 spectators witnessed the only two clubs to have completed the Double bring the curtain down on an exceptional footballing year.

Villa fielded the same eleven that carried off the FA Cup but the North End gave outings to four reserves in their forward line. These new boys were obviously anxious to make an impression, but no one else seemed keen to over-stretch themselves in this low-key affair.

The visitors attacked down the Deepdale slope in the first half and within seconds James Trainer had got down well to stop an excellent Wheldon shot. Meanwhile, at the other end, Spencer and Evans found themselves with plenty to do against Preston's inexperienced front rank. Brown, especially, caused problems, one shot of his grazing the bar.

A quick break down the right by Athersmith led to a Devey shot bound for the bottom corner. However, Trainer - ever a thorn in Villa's side - produced a miracle save, scooping the ball to safety.

The game speeded up towards half-time with the home side looking the stronger. It was the Villa, though, who finally broke the deadlock. Spencer floated in one of his stunning free-kicks into the path of Fred Wheldon who scored the last goal of the 1896/7 season.

In the second half, both 'keepers played well. Preston managed to cut out most of the supply to Athersmith, but Villa's left flank came more into the game. The last 15 minutes saw the home side press for an equaliser, but Whitehouse was cool under pressure and rounded off his season with a cleansheet and an impressive display. Thus Villa ran out 1-0 winners and extended their unbeaten run in first-class matches to eighteen games, five of which had been against Preston.

* * *

There was still some more football left in the weary Villa legs. On 28th April they entertained West Brom at the Lower Grounds in a poorly attended benefit for the players. Two goals from Devey and one from Wheldon secured a 3-1 victory. The next day Villa travelled to Notts County to play a benefit match, winning that 2-1. Twenty-four hours later came Walsall's victory in the Mayor's Cup

April 1897 had seen Aston Villa play three League matches, triumph in the FA Cup Final, play in two more Final-ties, and take the field for three friendly matches. In the final week of the month, they had played no less than five times.

At last the football had ended and the players could hang up their boots for the summer. There can be no doubt that they deserved their break. Having rounded off their League campaign in style, despite having nothing left to play for in the last three games, everyone connected with Aston Villa Football Club could feel justifiably proud of the lay-out of the final League table - a just reflection of the merits of that 1896/7 side:

		home					away						
	pld	w	d	l	f	a	w	d	l	f	a	g.av	pts
1 Aston Villa	30	10	3	2	36	16	11	2	2	37	22	1.92	47
2 Sheff U	30	6	4	5	22	16	7	6	2	20	13	1.45	36
3 Derby	30	10	2	3	45	22	6	2	7	25	28	1.40	36
4 Preston	30	8	4	3	35	21	3	8	4	20	19	1.38	34
5 Liverpool	30	7	6	2	25	10	5	3	7	21	28	1.21	33
6 Sheff W	30	9	4	2	29	11	1	7	7	13	26	1.14	31
7 Everton	30	8	1	6	42	29	6	2	7	20	28	1.09	31
8 Bolton	30	7	3	5	22	18	5	3	7	18	25	0.93	30
9 Bury	30	7	5	3	25	15	3	5	7	14	29	0.89	30
10 Wolves	30	6	4	5	26	14	5	2	8	19	27	1.10	28
11 N Forest	30	8	3	4	30	16	1	5	9	14	33	0.90	26
12 W Brom	30	7	2	6	18	16	3	4	8	15	40	0.59	26
13 Stoke	30	8	3	4	30	18	3	0	12	18	41	0.81	25
14 Blackburn	30	8	1	6	27	25	3	2	10	8	37	0.56	25
15 Sunderland	30	4	6	5	21	21	3	3	9	13	26	0.72	23
16 Burnley	30	4	5	6	25	25	2	2	11	18	36	0.70	19

Villa had thus equalled Sunderland's record of three League titles. But, as the table shows, they didn't just win the League - they steamrollered it!

Villa had more wins and fewer defeats than any other side by quite some margin. They were top scorers. They had easily the highest goal average, netting almost twice as many goals as they conceded. And, of course, their cushion at the top was a massive eleven points. This means that Villa's nearest rivals would have had to win an additional six matches in a thirty game season to overhaul the Champions. Rarely has such an incredible record been matched.

It is sometimes claimed that it was easier to win trophies in the years before football's modern era. But if that is so, how can one explain the fact that in the 71 years following the advent of the League, the Double was achieved only twice, yet in the most recent 35 seasons, there have been no less than five Double winners? Statistics may not show the full picture, but they do present interesting questions.

* * *

The Double winning Aston Villa were generally regarded as the finest team ever assembled, with only Glasgow's famous old Queen's Park side of the 1880's coming close. Much of this was put down to the tremendous team spirit which existed first at Perry Barr and then at Aston.

That spirit could not, however, prevent the departure of Campbell, Reynolds and Welford to Celtic, leaving Ramsay with the task of re-building - a task he completed very successfully. But the rest of the all-conquering immediately pledged their future to the Club.

The last time the players re-grouped before launching the defence of their title came on mid-summer's day when the Lower Grounds played host to a cycling and athletics event in honour of the Queen's Diamond Jubilee. It was here that Charlie Athersmith won the last two honours of what must surely be the most successful year ever enjoyed by any sportsman, at any time, anywhere in the world.

A 300 yard race had been set up between Villa's wing-wizard and S. Shepherd of Rochdale. £20 was on offer to the winner. Shepherd matched Charlie until the final bend when our man hit the accelerator to win comfortably in an amazing time of under 32 seconds. He then got his breath back and went and beat his team-mates, covering 220 yards in a little under 23 seconds. So the season ended in the same vein as it had progressed since September 1896 - Villa winning and Athersmith on a different planet.

Epilogue

A record season on the pitch was mirrored in the accounts. Despite building Villa Park and paying rent on two sites, 1896/7 proved to be Aston Villa's most financially rewarding year since its birth. Every part of the Club was running smoothly.

The gate money had risen by £3,368 compared with the previous year, primarily due to FA Cup exploits, and £1,000 was raised from non football interests. Predictions for the following year's income included £500 from hiring out the cycle track, and £250 from advertising hoardings. Sponsorship was expected to bring in a further £100, whilst the hosting of representative matches at Villa Park would add at least £150 to the kitty.

The Double season saw Aston Villa's income reach almost £11,000, well over a third of which was spent on players' wages. There had been some criticism in the press regarding the high win bonuses offered to the Villa squad. For the year as a whole, these amounted to £621 7s. 6d. A further £1,100 was spent on travelling, training camps and hotel accommodation.

But despite the massive costs of running the premier professional football club in the world, the Board were able to announce record profits of £1,300. All in all, it seems that Aston Villa enjoyed the perfect season in 1896/7. The Club even managed to raise over £1,000 for charity, thus keeping up its tradition of benevolence.

Aston Villa geared up for the new campaign knowing that they had lost the services of Messrs Campbell, Welford and Reynolds. That, along with the injury to Spencer, which wiped out almost the whole season for the Prince of Full-Backs, had much to do with Villa's trophy-less 1897/8.

Back to winning ways as the Century turned, Villa enjoying a further two League titles. Nothing, though, quite compared with that marvellous Double. They came close to repeating the feat on more than one occasion. The Championship of 1900 was secured but the Lions suffered quarter-final defeat in the Cup following a three-game struggle against Millwall. In 1903, semi-final defeat and a League runners-up spot left the Club empty-handed despite producing a fine campaign.

The 1905 Cup win coincided with an end of season run of 16 wins from 24 matches, but a poor start to the campaign meant only 4th place was achieved. Further League honours arrived in 1910 before the epic year long battle with Sunderland saw Villa take the Cup only to finish second to their rivals in the race for the title. A year later and another second placing and defeat in the semi-final.

After the Great War, however, Aston Villa lost their lead over the rest of football. With the Old Guard replaced by less visionary leaders, the Club slipped into mediocrity, with the eventual result being relegation. This prompted the return of Fred Rinder - and very nearly another amazing achievement. In 1938, as the Club stormed to the Second Division title, their hopes of FA Cup success were dashed at the semi-final stage by Preston North End. This was repeated in 1960, with Wolves ending Villa's Cup hopes.

Despite the continued Claret and Blue dominance of the game right up until the First World War, and the occasional excellent seasons since, one has to look as far as 26th May 1982 to find a day which could begin to match 10th April 1897. The European Cup Final defeat of Bayern Munich - whilst not being a brilliant game - was in the fine tradition of Devey's Double.

It was asserted at the beginning of this book that five key elements led to Villa's outstanding success of a Century ago. The same was true in 1982. The passion was evident, especially in players like Des Bremner, Dennis Mortimer, Ken McNaught, Allan Evans and Peter Withe. Luck too - just think of Rummenigge's inability to convert numerous golden chances. Vision and planning were provided by Ron Saunders who broke up a very good side in the late 1970's, replacing it with an even better team whilst other, less skilled observers, questioned his actions. And, of course, there was the pure, raw talent of Rimmer, Swain, Williams, Morley and, most notably of all, Cowans and Shaw.

But even the triumph in Europe doesn't quite equal the greatest success of the Rinder/Ramsay era. Tony Barton and his boys were allowed to leave the Club but their replacements were never found. Villa have had some great players and managerial success stories since the early 1980's, but never in a big enough number to lead to a continuity of success; something all Villa fans still regard as their birthright.

That belief (perhaps even arrogance) has its roots in the achievements of Victorian Villa. Back then, the Club was the undisputed King of Football. It enjoyed a run of sustained success which only three clubs (Arsenal, Manchester United and Liverpool) have since emulated. Thus, it is not hard to justify these words which were written in 1905:

"If there is a club in the country which deserves to be dubbed the greatest (and the matter is one of some delicacy), few will deny the right of Aston Villa to share the highest niche of fame with even the most historic of other aspirants. For brilliancy and, at the same time, for consistency of achievement, for activity in philanthropic enterprise, for astuteness of management, and for general alertness, the superiors of Aston Villa cannot be found."

So next time a Villa fan waxes lyrical about the greatness of his beloved Club, with little or no regard to how well they may have fared at the time of his outburst, remember that the Titan of which he speaks was created and nurtured over a Century ago. And no matter whether times be good or bad in 'Birmingham 6', that grandeur will never be diminished.

Aston Villa Football Club, and those early pioneers who are celebrated in this book, gave football a League and, with it, a future. Aston Villa brought glamour to a fledgling working class pastime. Aston Villa developed the stylish elegant play which is so highly lauded today. Aston Villa set the highest standards both on and off the field - the benchmark of footballing greatness.

Aston Villa: Double Winners 1897... and much, much more!

Appendix

Aston Villa's First-Class Record - Season 1896/7

Date	Versus	Comp.	Score	Scorers	Att.
02.09.96	STOKE CITY	Lge	2-1	John Cowan, Devey	6,000
05.09.96	West Brom.	Lge	1-3	Devey	12,000
12.09.96	SHEFFIELD UNITED	Lge.	2-2	Burton, Wheldon	5,000
19.09.96	Everton	Lge	3-2	Devey, Campbell 2	25,000
26.09.96	EVERTON	Lge	1-2	Devey	20,000
03.10.96	Sheffield United	Lge.	0-0		12,000
10.10.96	WEST BROM.	Lge	2-0	Wheldon, Campbell	18,000
17.10.96	Derby County	Lge	3-1	Wheldon, Campbell, John Cowan	8,500
24.10.96	DERBY COUNTY	Lge	2-1	John Cowan, Wheldon	10,000
31.10.96	Stoke City	Lge	2-0	Wheldon, Smith	6,000
07.11.96	BURY	Lge	1-1	Athersmith	5,000
14.11.96	Sheffield Wed.	Lge	3-1	Wheldon, Campbell, Athersmith	8,000
21.11.96	SHEFFIELD WED.	Lge	4-0	Smith, Athersmith, Devey, Wheldon	14,000
28.11.96	Blackburn R.	Lge	5-1	Devey, og, Smith, Wheldon, Campbell	7,000
19.12.96	NOTTINGHAM F.	Lge	3-2	Reynolds, Devey, Athersmith	7,000
25.12.96	Liverpool	Lge	3-3	Jas Cowan, Wheldon, Athersmith	25,000
26.12.96	Wolves	Lge	2-1	Chatt, Athersmith	18,000
02.01.97	BURNLEY	Lge	0-3		14,000
09.01.97	Sunderland	Lge	2-4	og, Campbell	8,000
16.01.97	SUNDERLAND	Lge	2-1	Wheldon, Devey	15,000
30.01.97	NEWCASTLE UTD.	FAC1	5-0	Athersmith, Wheldon 2, Smith, og	6,000
06.02.97	Bury	Lge	2-0	Campbell 2	10,000
08.02.97	Burnley	Lge	4-3	Campbell 3, Devey	5,000
13.02.97	NOTTS COUNTY	FAC2	2-1	Wheldon, Campbell	4,000
22.02.97	PRESTON N.E.	Lge	3-1	Devey 2, Athersmith	20,000
27.02.97	Preston N.E.	FAC3	1-1	Campbell	15,500
03.03.97	PRESTON N.E.	FAC3/R	0-0		12,000
06.03.97	Nottingham F.	Lge	4-2	Devey 2, John Cowan, Wheldon	8,000
10.03.97	Preston N.E.*	FAC3/2R	3-2	Athersmith 2, Campbell	22,000
13.03.97	LIVERPOOL	Lge	0-0		20,000
20.03.97	Liverpool*	FACSF	3-0	John Cowan, Wheldon, Athersmith	30,000
22.03.97	BOLTON W.	Lge	6-2	Athersmith, Reynolds, Campbell Wheldon 2, Devey	8,000
27.03.97	Bolton W.	Lge	2-1	Wheldon, Devey	7,000
10.04.97	Everton⁺	FACF	3-2	Campbell, Wheldon, Crabtree	65,891
17.04.97	BLACKBURN R.	Lge	3-0	Campbell, Wheldon, og	15,000
19.04.97	WOLVES	Lge	5-0	John Cowan 2, Devey, Campbell 2	50,000
26.04.97	Preston N.E.	Lge	1-0	Wheldon	3,000

Home matches in capitals. * - at Bramall Lane. ⁺ - at Crystal Palace.

Average home attendance (League only) -   Wellington Road: 12,462;
Aston Lower Grounds: 32,500;
Total: 15,133.

Player	League Apps.	League Gls.	FA Cup Apps.	FA Cup Gls.
CHARLIE ATHERSMITH	30	8	7	4
Frank Burton	8	1	-	-
John Campbell	29	16	7	4
Bob Chatt	11	1	1	-
JAS COWAN	30	1	7	-
John Cowan	15	6	3	1
James Crabtree	25	-	6	1
John Devey	29	16	7	-
Albert Evans	15	-	7	-
Jeremiah Griffiths	1	-	1	-
John Reynolds	24	2	6	-
Steve Smith	15	3	4	1
Howard Spencer	28	-	7	-
James Welford	10	-	-	-
FRED WHELDON (Top Scorer)	30	16	7	6
James Whitehouse	22	-	2	-
Tom Wilkes	8	-	5	-
own goals		3		1

(Ever-present players in capitals.)

Index